"I Can't Wait Till Sunday Morning!"

"I Can't Wait Till Sunday Morning!"

Creative Ideas to Enhance Your Children's Ministries

By
Evangelist Ed Dunlop

Illustrated by
Rebecca Dunlop

SWORD of the LORD
PUBLISHERS

P. O. BOX 1099, MURFREESBORO, TN 37133

Printed and Bound in the United States of America

To my mother, who led me to Jesus

With appreciation to Gary Beadles
and Evangelist Dale Grisso
for their prayers and advice
in the writing of this book

A special thank you to my daughter, Rebecca,
who did most of the artwork

Table of Contents

INTRODUCTION

"We need some workers in Children's Church, and we could really use your help," our bus director said, hopefully eyeing the group of young college students. "You'll be working with veteran teachers, and they'll help train you.

"Are any of you interested?"

Hesitantly, I raised my hand, not really sure what I was getting into. Sixteen years old, I had just left home weeks before and was struggling with the first semester of Bible college. Timid and shy, I was not at all sure that God could use an introvert like me, but my offer was accepted, and I was assigned to a Primary Church with a hundred fifty rowdy third graders.

Twenty-four years later, I can say that volunteering for Children's Church was just about the best decision I've ever made. It opened the door to some of the biggest blessings in my entire life.

Today's Primaries and Juniors Need...

...to be loved unconditionally.
...to be shown their need of a Saviour.
...to be led to receive Jesus as their Saviour.
...to be challenged to serve the Lord.
...to be taught that they are important to God.

I love Children's Church. For more than two decades, I've spent nearly every Sunday morning teaching the Bible to Primaries and Juniors. There's no place I'd rather be.

Bible college really didn't train me for this ministry, but I've watched some veteran teachers, read every book on teaching that I could get my hands on, and asked God to teach me. The Lord has blessed our ministry, and my wife and I have seen many, many children brought to Him through the ministry of Children's Church.

I want to share some of our ideas with you, and I trust that they will be a help and encouragement to your ministry. If nothing else, I trust that this book will challenge you to give your very best always, to seek to learn, grow and improve, always to be on the lookout for new ideas and better ways to present the message of Jesus to "your kids." The purpose of this book is to help you **improve** your ministry. It's a "how-to" manual, a resource of teaching ideas both for the beginning teacher and the veteran, but it's not filled with a lot of heavy educational philosophy.

As I use the term *Children's Church* (sometimes called "Junior Church") in this book, I'm referring to a Children's Church program for Primaries (first through third grades) and Juniors (fourth through sixth grades). Many of the ideas presented in the following pages can also be used with Beginners (four- and five-year-olds), and with Junior High students. And although this is a book for Children's Church workers, many of the ideas and concepts can be applied to Sunday school or any other children's ministries.

God bless you in your ministry to the children. Always, always, always give your very best! Allow me to paraphrase a familiar poem:

Good, better, best–

Never let it rest

'Til your Junior Church is better,

And you always give your best!

Meet Cindy Teachme and Joey Anykid, two of the youngsters in any Junior Church. Their backgrounds are radically different, yet many of their needs are the same. These kids deserve your very best!

Cindy is the eight-year-old daughter of the chairman of the deacon board. She's been in church all her life and knows more Bible verses than the average pastor. She claims to be a Christian yet has never really learned to apply her memory verses to her life. Like her mother, she's a bit disdainful of the "bus kids."

At first glance, Cindy would seem to be a very cooperative student and a real help in class. But as you get to know her, you find that she quietly works behind the scenes to stir up trouble, then places the blame on others.

Can you reach her for Christ?

Joey has been riding the church bus for nearly three years. He doesn't have a dad, and he lives with his alcoholic mother and two younger sisters. He's in third grade, but he's quick to remind you, "I'm supposed to be in fifth."

Joey received Jesus the third Sunday he came in your Junior Church, and he hasn't missed a Sunday since. He's still full of energy and at times can be a real problem in class. But he's learning and growing, and he loves Junior Church with all his heart. He makes it a point to hug you before he gets on the bus. With your help and encouragement, he'll grow up to serve God faithfully.

Like Cindy and Joey, the children in your Junior Church will have very diverse backgrounds and have a variety of needs. A quality Junior Church program is one that meets the students' needs. Ask God to use you and your workers to meet the needs of the kids to whom you minister.

1.

THE MINISTRY OF CHILDREN'S CHURCH

Imagine that your ten-year-old daughter has a brain tumor and needs emergency surgery to save her life. On the morning of the operation you meet the surgeon, a good-looking young doctor with a friendly smile. "Relax," he assures you. "Your little girl will do just fine. This operation will be a breeze!"

However, in talking further with the doctor you learn that he has never before attempted this type of surgery. Even worse, he has not done anything to prepare himself for the delicate, life-or-death operation ahead. He has not even taken the time to glance at your daughter's X rays or scans! "It's nearly twenty minutes 'til the surgery is scheduled," he tells you. "I'll just dash over to the hospital library and brush up on procedure from one of the medical journals."

Would you trust your child to a doctor who takes such a nonchalant attitude toward her life? I hope not! There's too much at stake!

The job of the Children's Church teacher is just as crucial as that of a brain surgeon! Dare we go into class unprepared or give less than our best? Eternal souls are at stake! Consider the words of Isaiah, and note the emphasis God places upon the teaching of children:

> **And all thy children shall be taught of the Lord; and great shall be the peace of thy children.**
> **Isaiah 54:13**

Consider the words of Jesus Himself in Matthew 18, a passage that deals with the importance of reaching children. In this great text the Saviour tells the story of the lost sheep (the parable of the ninety and

1

nine) and then makes this compelling statement:

Even so it is not the will of your Father which is in heaven, that one of these little ones should perish.

Matthew 18:14

Allow the words of the Saviour to touch your heart. Children are important to Jesus. He places great emphasis on the need to reach them with the Gospel. I firmly believe that your Children's Church is a ministry that's very close to the heart of God. Consider the words of Jesus in the next chapter of Matthew, same verse number:

But Jesus said, Suffer little children, and forbid them not, to come unto me: for of such is the kingdom of heaven.

Matthew 19:14

If children are important to Almighty God, shouldn't they be important to us? Consider this: *Your ministry in Children's Church on Sunday morning is just as important to God as your pastor's ministry in the adult service in the church sanctuary.* The children of your church are every bit as important as the adults.

If Jesus were to visit your church in person next Sunday morning, perhaps He wouldn't even bother to enter the main auditorium to hear your pastor! You might just find Him in Children's Church with the kids!

Never become complacent and satisfied with your own teaching. Always strive for excellence; seek constantly to improve; search for ways to present your vital message more effectively. A Children's Church teacher who is not learning and growing is regressing and becoming less effective.

The Objectives of Children's Church

As we seek to improve our Children's Church, let's first consider the objectives of this ministry: **evangelism**, **training** and **worship**. Our Children's Church should seek to **evangelize** children with the Gospel of Jesus Christ and lead them to receive Him as Saviour. Then we should be concerned with **training** these young believers and instructing them to serve the Lord.

Junior Church Objectives

1. Evangelism
2. Training
3. Worship

A third aspect of our ministry is **worship**. A Children's Church service should always be a worship service in which teachers and students alike praise and worship the Lord.

Every part of your Children's Church service should lend itself to one of these three main objectives.

Briefly, let's take a look at these three objectives of our ministry. First of all, **evangelism**—the best time to reach people with the Gospel is when they are young. Most people who receive Jesus as Saviour do so during childhood.

A number of years ago a survey was conducted in local churches across the nation. Church members were asked at what age they had responded to the Gospel. The results were amazing. According to this survey, eighty-five percent of the people who have accepted Christ did so between the ages of five and fourteen!

Obviously, the most fertile ground for the seed of the Gospel is the heart of a child! The best time to reach people for the Saviour is while they are young and their hearts are still tender. If we wait until adulthood to present the Gospel, in most cases the fertile ground of a child's heart has become hardened, and the claims of Jesus Christ are rejected. We must present the Gospel to children! One of the most important aspects of the Children's Church ministry is presenting God's way of salvation to young souls who need the Saviour.

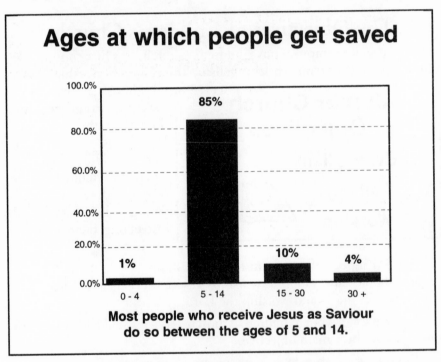

Ages at which people get saved

**Most people who receive Jesus as Saviour
do so between the ages of 5 and 14.**

There are those who do not believe that children can understand the Gospel and make a genuine decision to receive Him as Saviour. These people are not familiar with Matthew 18 and other Scripture passages in which Jesus taught that young children can believe and receive Him by faith. Charles Haddon Spurgeon, the great London preacher of the nineteenth century, once said, "Even a child of five, if properly instructed, can as truly believe and be regenerated as an adult."

My own mother led me to Christ before I was old enough to start school, but my parents had been careful to lay a Bible foundation for my decision, teaching Scripture to me twice a day from the time I was born. When I made the decision to ask Jesus to save me, the decision was my own.

Your Primaries and Juniors are old enough to receive Christ as Saviour. Present the gospel message clearly, pray for God's working in their hearts, but do not pressure them into a decision. Allow the Holy Spirit

> **"Even a child of five, if properly instructed, can as truly believe and be regenerated as an adult."**
> **--Charles Spurgeon**

to draw them to the Saviour, and the results will be real.

Again, one of the most important elements of the Children's Church ministry is **evangelism**.

The second major objective of your ministry is **training**. Once your students have come to know Jesus as Saviour, you want to train them to serve Him. Primaries and Juniors can be taught to walk with the Lord, to memorize and obey His Word, to be witnesses for Him, and to live in victory over sin and temptation. Children, like the rest of us, must be taught.

I often hear people say, "Our children are the church of tomorrow." The first time I heard this statement, I heartily agreed. Our children are important to God and to our churches. They are our future. When we are gone, it will be our children who will carry our faith to future generations.

> **"Our children are the church of tomorrow."**

But the above statement implies that we must train our young people now so that they may serve the Lord at some future date. Our children can be trained to serve the Lord now, while they are young. They do not have to wait until they reach adulthood to live for God. Some of the best Christians I have ever met were Primaries and Juniors.

"Our children are the church of ~~tomorrow~~." today

I would like to submit that *our children are the church of today.*

A third vital component of our Children's Church ministry is **worship**. The kids to whom we minister can be taught to worship our Lord. Every song, every prayer, every Children's Church offering and every Bible lesson is an act of worship, and we must make this clear to our students. Our Saviour delights in the worship of children as fully as He does in the worship of adults.

Again, the three main objectives of our Children's Church ministry are **evangelism, training** and **worship**. Every part of our program should lead naturally into accomplishing one or more of these three.

The Atmosphere of Children's Church

Let me hasten to say that the Children's Church service is not just a service for miniature adults. Kids are not little adults; they learn in different ways and have different needs than adults. The Children's Church service needs to be tailored to the needs of the kids and incorporate teaching at their level.

Today's Primaries and Juniors Need...

...teachers who are gentle, yet firm.
...teachers who model consistent Christianity.
...teachers who pray for them daily.
...teachers who always give their best.

The Children's Church program ought to be enjoyable for the students. If you're not afraid of the word, it ought to be *fun*.

Please notice that I did not say "nonsense" or "foolishness." I've observed far too many Children's Churches that were just that—nonsense and foolishness: puppets blowing their noses on a leader's clothes, then being threatened with bodily harm, workers getting doused with buckets of water, screaming contests for the sake of noise; and finally, a leader stands up after all the nonsense and shouts, "Now get quiet and listen to the lesson! This is the Word of God, and you're going to respect it!"

That's not at all what I have in mind when I say "fun." Kids can have fun listening to a well-told Bible story in which the storyteller makes use of voice techniques and visual aids. They can have fun competing in a Bible review game, or participating in a Sword drill, or even working on a memory verse. They can have fun singing praises to the Lord, watching an appropriate teaching video, or listening to a captivating missionary story.

What I'm saying is this: Children's Church ought to be planned with the students in mind and presented in such a way that they will be drawn into the activities and enjoy them.

I've been in Children's Churches that were simply replicas of the adult services taking place in the church sanctuary. Hymns are sung from church hymnals. A preacher stands and preaches a forty-five-minute message that would bore the sturdiest adults, and the boredom among the kids is so stiff you could cut it with the proverbial knife.

Last Sunday I heard a man complain, "When we bring kids in on the buses, they come only one time, and then they don't want to come back. The teachers aren't prepared for them, and the kids think it's dull and boring."

It shouldn't be that way! The Children's Church service ought to be so well-prepared, so interesting, and so exciting that the students just can't wait for Sunday morning to come!

Before we conclude this introductory chapter, let's take a look at how we divide the various age groups. This is the area where many churches make their biggest mistake. DO NOT PUT FOUR-YEAR-OLDS IN THE SAME CHILDREN'S CHURCH WITH TWELVE-

YEAR-OLDS AND EXPECT TO HAVE A QUALITY PROGRAM.

Take a look at the age divisions chart. If you have enough qualified workers, it's best to divide your children's departments into four divisions: Nursery (two- and three-year-olds), Beginners (four- and five-year-olds), Primaries (first through third grades), and Juniors (fourth through sixth grades). This is, of course, the ideal situation, but most churches do not have enough willing workers to staff four different children's churches.

Now take a look at the right-hand section of the chart. If you do not have enough workers for four separate children's churches, I suggest putting the two- and three-year-olds in the church nursery during the morning service and staffing two children's churches for the other ages. The Beginner Church would be for the four- and five-year-olds, while Children's Church would minister to the Primaries and Juniors.

Age Divisions

Ideal	Practical
2's and 3's	Nursery (2's & 3's)
Beginners	Beginners
Primaries	Primaries/Juniors
Juniors	

Don't try to put four-year-olds in with sixth-grade students. It just doesn't work. There is more difference in the attention span, vocabulary and thinking skills of a four-year-old and a sixth grader than there is between a sixth grader and a college graduate.

If you try to span too many ages in one class, one of two things will happen. Either you'll gear the program to the younger ones and bore the older ones, or you'll reach the older ones and lose the little ones. Either way, you're asking for trouble. The group that's bored will not just sit idle; they'll cause problems.

Time after time I've had teachers tell me, "We have kids from age four to twelve in our Children's Church, and it works out just fine!" Moments later, they're saying, "But we're having a lot of discipline problems. Can you help us?" Somehow they just can't see the problems created by combining the Juniors with the Beginners.

> Last week Phillip brought his sister Marcie to Junior Church. She's only four. Marcie wet her pants and started crying during the Bible story. We never did hear the end of the story!

Keep the age groups separate. Primaries and Juniors work well together in Children's Church, but don't try to include the Beginners.

Every Junior Church Leader Should . . .
. . . know Jesus Christ as personal Saviour.
. . . be dedicated to living for Christ.
. . . believe that kids are important to God.

I trust that you're EXCITED about your Children's Church ministry! Always give your very best. In the next chapter, we'll take a look at how to schedule a Children's Church program with enough VARIETY to hold the students' attention.

10 Ways to Establish Rapport With Your Students

1. Be available before and after class.

2. Listen when your students talk.

3. Learn each child's name and use it frequently.

4. Visit in the home. Get to know the family.

5. Send cards and letters. Kids love to get mail!

6. Attend their ball games, recitals, etc.

7. Send birthday cards.

8. Plan Junior Church outings.

9. Make phone calls to remind students of contests, outings, etc.

10. Pray for each child daily.

Ask Andy!

Dear Andy,

The kids in our Children's Church seem to have real bladder problems. We can hardly make it through the song service without six or eight kids having to be excused to use the rest room, and by the time we get into the Bible lesson, it's a regular parade, with one kid after another marching out. Needless to say, it's a real distraction. Any suggestions?

Jim Nasium

Dear Jim,

Glad you asked—this is a common problem in many Children's Churches. It also has a very simple solution: start by making sure that there is time for a brief restroom break between Sunday school and Children's Church. Give an opportunity for the kids who really have to go.

Once Children's Church starts, conclude your behavior announcement by saying, "If you think you have to go to the rest room during church, be sure that it's a real emergency before you go. Because if you go, it's gonna cost you! When you come back in, Mr. Williams will make you sit in the back, and you won't be able to see as well. Also, if you go, you automatically lose your chance for *Let's Make a Deal!* If I were you, I wouldn't go unless I really had to!"

Be consistent about enforcing this rule, and you'll be

surprised how fast the rest-room parade will stop.

Best wishes,

Andy

Dear Andy,

Our church runs several vans and buses. Some of our bus riders try to bring younger brothers and sisters into Children's Church, even though they are too young. They always use the excuse, "Mom says we have to stay together."

The little ones are always a distraction, but are we doing the right thing by sending them to their own class? If the parents want them to stay together, shouldn't we honor their wishes?

Polly Esther Fabric

Dear Polly,

How many times I've heard that same line from my Children's Church kids! Sometimes the kids are simply following instructions from home, but usually they're trying to pull a fast one.

The workers in our Children's Church have been trained to allow siblings to stay together, but both kids have to go to the younger one's class! You'd be amazed at how fast the older brother or sister decides to let the little one go to his own class where he belongs! Hope this helps!

Andy

Dear Andy,

Our church refuses to buy any lesson visuals or equipment for our Junior Church. Whenever we approach the pastor or the finance committee with a need, we always hear, "There's no money in the budget for that."

How can we get our church to supply the necessary materials to do a decent job of teaching these kids?

I. Ben Wonduron

Dear Ben,

I've been there myself. Here are a couple of suggestions:

First, make an appointment with the pastor or finance committee to present your needs. Don't try to buttonhole them in the foyer after church—they're more apt to listen seriously if you go to the trouble to make an appointment.

Second, if you get nowhere in your meeting, why not begin to buy the needed items yourself? The church doesn't always have to pay for everything. Set aside some of your own money. Anytime you buy items with your own funds, be sure to mark them clearly with your name, and file your receipts so there's never any question of ownership should you move to another church (unless, of course, you choose to donate the materials).

A third idea might be to get permission to use your Junior Church offerings to purchase equipment and supplies. Then plan an offering contest among the kids to generate excitement for the project. Good luck!

Andy

2.
SCHEDULING THE PROGRAM

> ## Cindy sez:
> ## "I hate it when we have the same old thing every week in Junior Church!"

I love mushroom pizza. Just the thought of a piping hot pizza loaded with gobs of gooey Mozzarella cheese and plump mushrooms makes my mouth water. But after a pizza feast, I don't even want to see a pizza the next day. I sure don't want it for breakfast. I like VARIETY!

It's the same with Children's Church. No one wants to see or hear the same thing week after week, but everyone enjoys VARIETY!

Take a look at the sample Children's Church schedule. The service is one hour and twenty minutes, from 11:00 until 12:20. Notice that there is quite a bit of VARIETY; each activity in the program is brief and flows right into the next. The interest level of the students stays high because of the VARIETY. Let's quickly walk through the program.

Children's Church opens with a welcome to the students and then a brief, fun opener. This may be a game of "Simon Says." The opener might be a crowd stunt or a skit, but it's always something that's fun and gets the kids participating and laughing.

The **fun opener** is perhaps the only part of the program that has

> **Use VARIETY in scheduling your Junior Church program!**

> ### Sample Schedule (11:00-12:20)
> | | |
> |---|---|
> | 11:00 | Fun Opener *get them laughing* |
> | 11:05 | Songs - *quick lively songs* |
> | 11:10 | Memory Verse *- monthly* |
> | 11:15 | Songs *w/ offering sandwiched in* |
> | 11:20 | Missionary Story, Puppets, or Video *keeps with topic* |
> | 11:30 | Songs *slower + quieter* |
> | 11:35 | LESSON *conclude w/ an invitation* |
> | 12:00 | Bible Game *for review* |
> | 12:15 | Behavior Award |
> | 12:20 | Dismissal |

See pages 19 + 20

15

no spiritual teaching, but it does have a purpose: it welcomes the kids to Children's Church in a way that says, "We're glad you're here, and we hope you enjoy the service!" First-time visitors relax and begin to realize that they're in a place where people love them and believe that Children's Church ought to be enjoyed. The opener is brief, fun, and creates an atmosphere that is conducive to learning.

 The opener is followed by a short, but lively, **song time**. The Children's Church song leader should be an energetic, enthusiastic person who believes that when kids sing, they should really SING! Use kids' choruses and cheerful gospel songs. Many excellent visualized songs are available from Christian publishers.

This portion of the song service should be brief, perhaps three or four quick choruses. Have the kids stand for the first song, seated for the second, stand for the third, etc. Action choruses with motions are especially appropriate for the first segment of the song service.

The next item on your schedule is the **memory verse**. One of your workers comes forward and drills the memory verse for the month, visualizing it on the chalkboard or marker board, with the overhead projector or with flashcards. Methods for teaching and reviewing memory verses will be discussed in a later chapter.

But seek ye first the kingdom of God, and his righteousness; and all these things shall be added unto you.
Matthew 6:33

It's now 11:15 in your Children's Church, and the program calls for **more songs**. After one or two lively, cheerful songs, the Children's Church **offering** is taken, followed by another **song**.

This second song time can be followed by a **missionary story**, **puppets**, or perhaps an appropriate, short **video**. Again, use VARIETY. Your entire program should revolve around one teaching theme that will be developed in your lesson, so the puppet skit, object lesson or video should be centered around this same theme.

Somewhere around 11:30 you'll have a third **song time** planned. Your song leader should have the children stand again to sing, but the songs for this segment should be ones that are a little slower, calmer and quieter. The Bible message is to follow, and a good song leader can use the music to quiet the kids and prepare them for the message.

Now comes the most important part of the entire Children's Church hour—the **Bible lesson**. The entire program revolves around this message. Every song, puppet skit, object lesson or video should introduce or reinforce the truths that are presented in the Bible story. Of course, the Bible lesson will be shorter than the sermon presented in the adult worship service, but it is just as important as the adult sermon. The Junior Church message usually lasts twenty or twenty-five minutes, depending in part on how well the teacher holds the attention of the students. More will be said about the lesson in Chapter 4.

The Bible lesson concludes with an **invitation**, followed by a **Bible review game**. The review game is a time of active competition and class participation and is used to review and reinforce the truths taught in the Bible lesson. Bible games are one of the most exciting and effective teaching methods you will ever see and should be used by all teachers of Primaries and Juniors. Nine different Bible games are presented in Chapter 7.

The time in Children's Church has gone by quickly, and it's almost time to dismiss. One final part of the program still remains, and it's one the kids all look forward to: the **behavior awards**. Some of your workers have been keyed to watch for the best-behaved children during the entire service, and now it's time to announce the winners. As the winners are chosen, they come forward and receive their rewards.

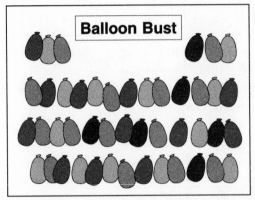

But the winners are not just handed a prize. Oh no; it's much more exciting than that! Today, we're playing **Let's Make a Deal**! Or perhaps it's **Balloon Bust Board**, or **The Mad Dash**! Our winners are going to compete in an exciting behavior award game and then be awarded their prizes. (See the behavior award games in Chapter 3.) Children's Church concludes on a happy, exciting note, and as the kids are dismissed, some of them don't seem to want to leave. Now, isn't that the way Children's Church should be?

Again, let me say that the key to planning a successful Children's Church program is VARIETY. No one likes to see the same old thing week after week, especially not the kids. I use ventriloquism, and kids fall in love with Andy, my little, talking friend, but I don't use ventriloquism every Sunday. I also use sleight of hand and special effects, but I don't use the same methods every week. I keep a written record of each Children's Church service and rotate the various methods and visuals for the sake of VARIETY.

Take a look at the alternate schedule on the next page. Notice how it varies from the first sample schedule. Some of the components in the early part of the service have been deleted, and the lesson has been moved up fifteen minutes, making room for a fifteen-minute video at the end of Children's Church.

Again, use VARIETY in planning your teaching schedule. You may not follow either of the sample schedules as I've presented them here, and your Children's Church program may include some components I haven't even mentioned, but I've included these examples to demonstrate the VARIETY that needs to be a part of your program.

(I write my Children's Church program schedule on a 12" x 16" marker board. At any point in the program, I can take a glance at the board and see how we are doing. If we are running behind schedule, I can eliminate a song or two, shorten the Bible game, etc. The schedule must be flexible.)

As you schedule your Children's Church program, be sure to use plenty of VARIETY! Keep the students interested and excited about learning! In the next chapter, we'll address the most difficult aspect of the Children's Church ministry.

Alternate Schedule
(11:00-12:20)

11:00 Puppets

11:05 Songs

11:10 Memory Verse

11:15 Songs

11:20 LESSON

11:45 Bible Game

12:00 Video

12:15 Behavior Award

12:20 Dismissal

See next page + page 13

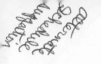

Evaluating the Children's Church Program

YES NO

___ ___ 1. Does my Children's Church program incorporate a VARIETY of teaching methods and activities?

___ ___ 2. Do the various parts of the program revolve around one central teaching aim, explained and developed in my lesson?

___ ___ 3. Are the transitions (from one activity to the next) smooth and natural?

___ ___ 4. Is my program fast-paced and interesting?

___ ___ 5. Do I have a minute-by-minute schedule so that the entire teaching hour is well-planned and organized?

___ ___ 6. Do I have my equipment and visuals so well-organized that there is no "dead air" as I move from one activity to the next?

___ ___ 7. Do I plan so well that my students never have to sit and wait while I focus a projector, cue a tape, etc.?

___ ___ 8. Do I keep a written record of each Children's Church service so I can keep track of the VARIETY of methods?

___ ___ 9. Am I willing to try new teaching methods?

___ ___ 10. If I were a Primary or Junior child, would I find my Children's Church program interesting and challenging?

Ask Andy!

Dear Andy,

Our church has a top-notch Children's Church program. Our workers are dedicated, caring people who pray regularly for the kids, spend much time in preparation, and do a fantastic job of teaching. They make and use some first-rate visuals, there's a lot of variety, and the lessons are superb. It's a joy to work with a group of people like these folks.

The problem is that some of the older kids (seventh and eighth grade) want to come to our Children's Church! They say that the adult service is boring, and they just don't get anything out of it. (They may have something there—we hear the same complaints from many adults.)

My question is this: Should we allow the older kids to come to Children's Church? Would we be sacrificing the program for the younger kids if we try to minister to the older ones? We're afraid that if we don't include the older ones, some of them will stop coming to church.

Sarah Bellum

Dear Sarah,

Thanks for your letter. I think many churches struggle with the same decision you are facing.

As I see it, you need to address two questions as you make your decision:

(1) Can we minister to these older kids more effectively in Children's Church than in the adult service? and

(2) Will the older kids be a detriment to our program

for the younger children?

In many of today's churches, the adult service is not geared to the needs of young people. Very few pastors use visual aids; some do not even use adequate illustrations! Often the message does not address the needs of the kids. Many Junior High kids (especially bus riders) simply lose interest and drop out. If your pastor is not on his toes in regard to communicating with these kids, a quality Children's Church program may very well do a better job of meeting their needs.

You may want to allow seventh and eighth graders in Children's Church on a trial basis. Let these students know up front that they are "on probation"—any individual who comes into Children's Church for any reason other than to learn and participate will be sent back into the adult service.

I've allowed Junior Highers to come into my Junior Church ministry (with caution), and we've had a fruitful ministry to these kids.

Andy

Dear Andy,

Several church families do not send their kids to our Children's Church; they keep them in the adult service. I think that our Children's Church program will minister to these kids better than the adult service.

What should we do?

Rusty Carr

Dear Rusty,

Don't feel insulted when parents refuse to let their children attend your Children's Church. These folks may have had a bad experience with Children's Church in another church.

Why not personally invite these parents (one couple at a time) to sit in on your Children's Church program one Sunday? If you have a quality program and the needs of the kids are being met, one visit ought to convince them that their kids would benefit from your teaching.

But if not, don't badger them.

Andy

Dear Andy,

How do you get the attention of a large group of children in order to start an activity or a service?

Standing up front and yelling, "Get quiet! Get quiet! Get quiet!" just doesn't seem to work. There must be a better way.

Any suggestions?

Pam Flit

Dear Pam,

There is a better way—get a cheer ball. Purchase a brightly-colored plastic or rubber ball about the size of a baseball or softball. Introduce the cheer ball to your group as a fun way to test their intelligence, alertness and reaction time. Explain that anytime you toss the ball into the air, they are to cheer ("yeah!") as long as the ball is in the air. The instant the ball lands back in your hand, they are to get quiet.

Have some fun with it! The first time you introduce the cheer ball concept, toss it up two or three times so they get the idea. Then have just the boys cheer, then just the girls, then just the adults, etc. (When it's the girls' turn, feint with the ball, but don't throw it up. The girls will cheer anyway, which gets a laugh from the boys. The next time you use the ball, trick the boys.)

Once your group is familiar with the cheer ball, you can use it to gain attention immediately. Simply pick up the ball and toss it up without announcing it. Even if the group is talking and disorderly, ten percent of the kids will see the ball and cheer. Half will cheer on the second toss, and everyone will cheer on the third toss. Then simply hold the ball as you make your announcement, give instructions or whatever, and you have the attention of the entire group! I've used it with groups of more than a thousand kids!

Don't overuse the cheer ball idea, and don't use it during the serious parts of the service (i.e., during the Bible lesson, etc.), but it can be a fun, effective way to call any group of children to order.

Try it—you'll like it!

Andy

3.

MAINTAINING DISCIPLINE IN CHILDREN'S CHURCH

Without a doubt, the biggest problem Children's Church teachers face is classroom control and discipline. If you hang around after Children's Church, you'll often hear:

"These kids are so unruly; how do I get them to listen?"

"Why can't these little monsters sit still for just one hour?"

"When our students come out of Sunday School, they are wound up and ready to move. We can't do anything with them in Children's Church."

Sound familiar? Perhaps you, like so many other teachers, feel that you have been called by God to work with kids, and yet you're just not sure how much more your nerves can handle. By the time you get home for Sunday dinner, you've practiced your resignation speech a hundred times, and shouldn't Children's Church teachers be drawing combat pay?

I quit! These kids are impossible!

I trust that this chapter will be a help and an encouragement to you. I've fought some of those same battles myself and know what it can be like, but I watch people and have learned some things from some veteran teachers. You **can learn** to maintain control of your Children's Church, no matter how large the group or how unruly the students may be. I'd like to share some things that I've learned. This just might be the most important chapter in the entire book.

I can't help but think of an assembly program I did last year in a public school in Mississippi. Eleven hundred elementary school children sat restlessly in the bleachers, waiting for the program to begin. As the principal began my introduction, I breathed a silent prayer, "Lord, give me the hearts and attention of these kids."

Moments later, I switched on my wireless mike and stepped out in front of that huge sea of eager faces, knowing that I had to capture the attention of every student in the first fifteen or twenty seconds. If I didn't, this drug and alcohol assembly would be a disaster.

An hour later, as the students filed quietly out of the gymnasium, a third-grade teacher approached me. "That was magnificent!" she gushed. "The students listened to every word you said! How did you do it?"

I thought about her question as the host pastor and I drove back to the church where we were holding the kids' crusade. How does a teacher maintain control in the classroom, especially since today's children are more unruly, undisciplined and troubled than any generation before them? Can today's Children's Church teacher even expect to achieve any semblance of order during class time?

The answer to the second question is a resounding "YES!" The first question will take a little more time to answer.

The teacher is the key to order in the classroom, and a teacher of God's Word must undertake that responsibility and use every resource available as he teaches. Here's how—

1. Pray

We must never forget that we are in a spiritual battle and that our adversary opposes the teaching of God's Word. Don't you think he knows how to stir up your students, creating disturbances and discipline problems, in order to minimize the effectiveness of the teaching of the Word?

Train your Children's Church workers to pray during the entire service. Ask some of your church parents to pray for your ministry every Sunday morning. Learn to pray as you teach, continually seeking God's help and blessing as you conduct the program.

Never stand before any group of children without first asking God to give you the full attention of every student. He can settle even the most unruly child. The battle is the Lord's.

2. Be Well-Prepared

Many discipline problems are simply the result of a lack of preparation. A teacher should know the lesson so thoroughly that he or she can teach with only an open Bible in hand, with no need to refer to the lesson manual or quarterly.

Arrive early. You should be in the Children's Church classroom long before the first student arrives. Before class begins, every visual aid should be in place, every visualized song chosen and placed in the order in which it will be used (with the sheet music already at the piano), every projector focused and ready to roll. The Bible review game should be set up before class, with a written list of questions nearby. Preparation is the key. Many times the battle is won or lost before class even begins.

Plan every minute of class time. Know in advance what is going to happen during every segment of your teaching time. Your lesson plan should include a schedule of every activity that will take place. Organization is vital to order and good discipline.

3. Teach With Enthusiasm!

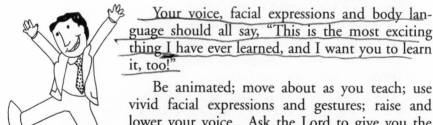

Your voice, facial expressions and body language should all say, "This is the most exciting thing I have ever learned, and I want you to learn it, too!"

Be animated; move about as you teach; use vivid facial expressions and gestures; raise and lower your voice. Ask the Lord to give you the enthusiasm you need to hold your students' attention. If you are truly excited about the lesson, your students will get excited, too.

4. Make Maximum Use of Visual Aids

"Seeing is believing." "A picture is worth a thousand words." The educators tell us that **seventy-five** percent of what we know came through our sense of sight, but only **thirteen** percent through our sense of hearing! They also tell us that we remember five times as much when we *see and hear* something, as opposed to hearing it alone.

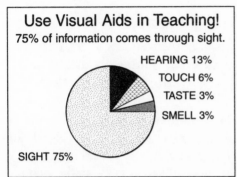

Use Visual Aids in Teaching!
75% of information comes through sight.

HEARING 13%
TOUCH 6%
TASTE 3%
SMELL 3%
SIGHT 75%

Do you want to be as effective as possible when you teach God's Word? Use visual aids as often as you can! Visuals grab the student's attention, help him to understand the lesson, and cause him to remember it.

In my drug and alcohol assemblies in the public elementary and junior high schools, I make use of a giant, 4' x 8' Velcro board. In just one presentation, I use forty-eight different pictures and word cards on the Velcro board, a stuffed mouse and a real rat trap, an empty beer can and several "joints," and a whiskey bottle and half-burnt hat from a drinking party where five people died. The message has impact because of the visuals.

Have you watched television lately? In just one sixty-minute program, the Devil spends several million dollars on his visuals! He knows their effectiveness. We can't match him dollar for dollar, but shouldn't we as teachers of the Word learn to communicate our vital message as powerfully as possible?

If you use a Children's Church curriculum, please realize that you are not limited to the visuals that came in your lesson packet. Ask God to teach you to be creative! Find a new way to visualize the plan of salvation, every bit of your lesson (especially the application), your memory verses, your announcements, everything!

5. Practice Good Eye Contact

How true it is that the eyes are "the windows of the soul." The eyes of a teacher can be dynamic teaching tools, if he knows how to use them. His eyes can express excitement and anticipation as he teaches; they can radiate warmth and friendliness; they can portray sincerity and intense feeling. As he becomes involved with the characters of the Bible story, his eyes can portray rage, love, worry, disappointment, hatred, anxiety, compassion.

Learn to look into the eyes of the students as you teach. Give each child the impression that you are teaching directly to him. Often you can hold the attention of a class simply by practicing good eye contact with each student.

The eyes of the students are just as important. The pupils' eyes can provide you with all sorts of information, if you are alert enough to pick up on the signals. By watching your pupils' eyes, you can know immediately when they are becoming restless and you need a slight change of pace. You can tell when they are excited, when they are pleased, and when they are enjoying class. By observing the questions in a child's eyes, you become aware of the need to rephrase or explain a concept.

Use your eyes to help communicate your message to the students, and be sure to pick up the nonverbal signals they are sending you.

Many times discipline problems can be avoided simply by making eye contact with the student whose attention you have momentarily lost. Are those two little girls on the second row talking again during the lesson? Simply walk over and stand in front of them as you continue to teach. The moment you make eye contact with one or both of them, shake your head ever so slightly. They'll get the message. If they don't, stop and correct the problem.

Seat the students as close to you as possible. Kids don't take as much

The teacher is the key to order in Junior Church.

space as adults when they are seated. Place the rows of chairs a little closer together—you'll be amazed at how much closer the back row suddenly becomes.

Instead of arranging the chairs into six rows of five chairs each, why not have three rows of ten chairs each? Your eye contact with each student will improve dramatically as the students are brought closer to you.

6. Seat Your Workers Among the Students

Classroom control is always easier if your workers are seated among the children, rather than standing along the sides of the room or seated in the back. The immediate presence of an adult is a strong deterrent to disruptive behavior, and if a student does act up, the worker can handle the situation quietly and unobtrusively, without disturbing the rest of the class.

Train your workers to be alert for disturbances and disruptive behavior around them. Many problems can be corrected by a nonverbal message directed toward the errant student: a stern look, a slight shake of the head, or a finger held in front of the lips. If the misbehavior continues, the worker needs to move the student quietly to a seat beside an adult.

When a child becomes aggressive or confrontational, do not attempt to correct him or her in front of the group. Have a worker quietly remove the student from the classroom to deal with the situation privately. This worker should explain calmly but firmly why such behavior is disruptive to the class and why it cannot be tolerated. Address the behavior problem, but don't belittle or demean the student.

Once the problem is corrected, allow the student to return to the classroom to sit beside a worker at the back of the group.

7. Consider Rearranging Your Classroom

You don't have to keep the same room arrangement that the previous leaders had. Perhaps some rearranging would improve the efficiency of your teaching and improve class discipline as well. Many times teachers fail to realize just how much influence the classroom setting can have on the students' attention and behavior.

Look about your Children's Church room. Check out the lighting, the placement of the doors and windows, the way in which the rows of chairs are arranged. Is there a better way? Don't rearrange solely for the sake of change; but sometimes some simple changes in the classroom can make dramatic improvements in the teaching situation.

Take the placement of the classroom doors, for instance. Are they in the front or the side of the room, so that every latecomer or bathroom-parader is a major distraction as he slips in or out? Why not turn the chairs around so that they face the opposite wall and the classroom doors are behind the students? One such change, small as it is, can sometimes

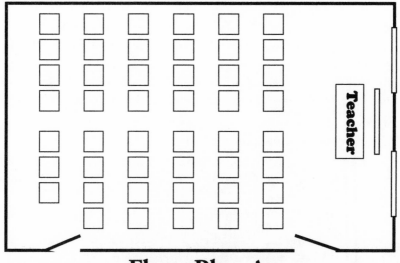

Floor Plan A

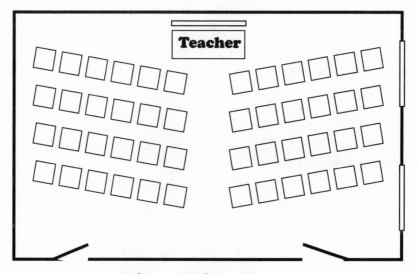

Floor Plan B

make a world of difference in the effectiveness of your teaching.

How about the classroom windows? Do you as the teacher stand with your back to them, so that the students are facing the glare as you teach, making it hard for them to see? Be aware of the various aspects of the classroom setting. They're more important than you might think.

One Saturday morning go down to the church, slip into your Children's Church room, and just sit in one of the pupils' chairs for a few minutes. Visualize your Children's Church program as you sit there, imagining it from the child's perspective. What changes should be made?

Consider the two different floor plans on the previous page, both for the same classroom. Floor Plan A utilizes six rows of chairs, with eight chairs in each row. As the children face the visual board at the front of the room, they are also facing two bright windows. The door at the front right corner of the room is sure to be a constant source of distraction.

Now look at Floor Plan B, same classroom, same seating for forty-eight students, but the chairs have been turned so that the kids now face the long wall, with the distraction of the doors behind them! The windows are now to the side, so there's no glare as the students face the teacher and his visual aids. Perhaps best of all, there are now only four rows of seats, instead of six. Think of how much closer the students on the back rows will be and how much more they will be involved in the Children's Church program!

Make your classroom work for you, instead of against you. At times the simplest changes in the room can make the greatest difference in the behavior of your students and in the effectiveness of your Children's Church.

Sometimes you can't change the situation, but you can work through the distractions and problems. If the students must face the windows, why not invest in some blinds or solar film or both? If for some reason you can't do anything about those doors that are such a distraction, why not at least hang a simple sign on the one that's the greatest problem?

8. Expect Good Behavior

Don't settle for anything less. Once you have given the rules (keep them brief and simple), enforce them and expect the students to follow them. It may take a few weeks, but even today's children can be trained to listen and follow orders. Many teachers simply don't expect their students to obey, and so the students live up to those expectations.

Joey sez:
"When Mr. Larson teaches, the kids really listen. He makes 'em! But when Mr. Davis teaches, the kids do what they want!"

9. Use Behavior Awards

Give the students a tangible reason for following your rules. Most children today, even those from Christian homes, are undisciplined. They're just not accustomed to doing something simply because an adult said so. By using behavior awards, you'll get the students going your way a lot quicker, and besides, the behavior awards are fun!

In my school assemblies, I use balloon sculptures. We ask at the office how many classes will attend the assembly, then make two balloons for each class.

After a fun time of illusions and ventriloquism to establish rapport with the students, I'm ready to get to the serious part of the program. I pick up a balloon and blow it up. As I twist the balloon into an animal shape, I tell the teachers (with the students listening), "Start watching right now for the quietest boy and the quietest girl in your class. At the end of the program come up and choose two balloon sculptures, one for each winner."

At that point I turn my attention back to the students. "If you want to win a balloon sculpture, just do two things: one, sit up straight; and two, no talking. Your teacher is choosing the best students in your class, and you could be one of the winners."

In order for behavior awards to be effective, they must be awarded on an individual basis. None of this "We're watching for the best row" business. It simply doesn't work. Every child knows that if one person in his row messes up, his own chance of winning evaporates along with the other child's.

Even less effective is the concept of the "quiet seat" or "secret seat" award. With this method, one chair is chosen by the teacher before class begins. If the student sitting in that seat is relatively well-behaved during the lesson, he or she receives a prize. If not, nobody receives the prize. This method is ineffective for this reason: every student quickly realizes that no matter how well he behaves during class, if he's not in the "lucky" seat, his chances of winning are nil.

Why not simply announce, "Today, class, we're watching for the best boy and the best girl in our class. Those two winners will be allowed to play a special game and win some prizes. If you want to be a winner, just follow two rules—number one, sit up straight; number two, no talking.

Right after our Bible game, we'll find out who today's winners are!"

The students will try harder to win the behavior contest if you make a game of presenting the prizes. Here are several ideas that we have used effectively over the years:

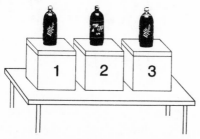

(a) **LET'S MAKE A DEAL.** Before your students arrive, place one or more prizes in each of three brightly painted wooden boxes with lids. The numerals 1, 2 and 3 should be stenciled on the front of the boxes. Shoe boxes or decorative lunch sacks with the numerals in Magic Marker will also work well. Two of the boxes contain desirable prizes, while the third contains a "whammy" (a diaper, potato or some other useless item).

As you teach, an unidentified worker, "secret agent," selects three winners from the class. Tell the students that one winner will be chosen from the boys, one from the girls, and that the third winner may be either a boy or girl.

During the last two or three minutes of class, play **Let's Make a Deal**. The three winners are each handed a prize, then given the option of keeping it or trading it for one of the boxes, not knowing, of course, what the boxes contain. Caution them in advance about the whammy. (If a child receives the whammy, give him an opportunity to trade back by choosing a number between one and three, etc. If he chooses the wrong number, be ready with a consolation prize after class.)

> ## Cindy sez:
> "Let's Make a Deal is my favorite!"
>

Let's Make a Deal has always been a winner, and I'm sure that your students will love it!

(b) THE PRICE IS RIGHT. Display several prizes on a table, with the price of each item concealed in a folded, stapled index card. Three or four winners guess the price of each item, with each prize going to the child who guesses closest to the price without going over. Set a prize limit in advance (three or four items) so that one child does not walk away with all the prizes. When a child reaches the limit, the game continues without him. Be ready with consolation prizes for the occasional child who is outguessed on every item.

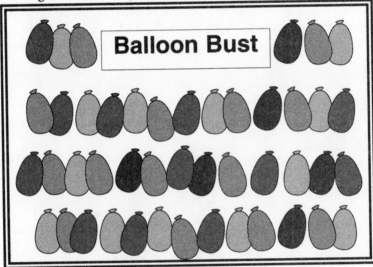

(c) BALLOON BUST BOARD. This is a winner with any group of Primaries or Juniors. Insert paper slips naming different prizes into a number of balloons, inflate them, then fasten them to a sheet of plywood or paneling with tape or thumbtacks. (Cluster the balloons toward the center of the board.)

The winners throw three or four darts from a short distance, receiving the prize named in any balloon they pop. Plan for each student to pop at least one or two balloons, and give them additional darts until they succeed.

Note: Use extreme caution with this game. Be certain that no spectators, including teachers, are anywhere near the target area. Children can be unbelievably wild with a dart. With a class of younger students, you might even consider taping a dart to the end of a 16-inch dowel rod and having the winners simply poke the balloons. Not quite as much fun, but a lot safer!

THE MAD DASH

(d) THE MAD DASH. This has been a favorite. Place a number of prizes on a table with a tape line on the floor ten or twelve feet away. Place three or four grocery sacks behind the line. At a given signal, the selected winners race to the table, grab one item each, then race back and drop them in their sacks. Taking only one item at a time, they collect as many prizes as they can in fifteen seconds!

Another form of **The Mad Dash** is to place six or eight simple tasks on the table for the winner to perform in thirty seconds (drinking a cup of water, stacking eight or ten blocks, threading a needle, etc.). Each time the child completes a task, he wins an additional prize. You can't possibly imagine the excitement this behavior game will generate!

(e) KING AND QUEEN. Purchase gold foil crowns at a toy store or discount house. Choose the best boy and girl in Children's

Church, then call them forward and crown them. (The child keeps the crown.) The **King and Queen** then get to choose a prize from your treasure chest.

This idea is very effective with Beginners, Primaries and younger Juniors, but the older Juniors may not get a real thrill out of it. Use **King and Queen** only if you have a class of younger students.

(f) **THE MYSTERY PRIZE.** This is a very simple idea, but if used correctly, can generate an unbelievable response. Place a very attractive prize (a bag of fun-size candy bars, six-pack of Coke or some other item that you **know** that the students will like) in a large, paper grocery sack, then staple the top securely closed. Draw a large question mark (?) on the front of the sack with a Magic Marker.

As you make your behavior award announcement at the opening of Children's Church, display the mystery sack. "Today, class, we are watching for just one winner! This person will receive..." (pause dramatically and hold up the sack) "the **Mystery Prize!** This bag contains something that I know you will just love! Would you like to see it?"

Pop open the top of the sack and peer inside, letting your eyes grow wide as you view the prize. Ham it up just a bit. "I mean, this prize is awesome! Mr. Jenkins, would you like to see the **Mystery Prize?**" (Call one of your workers forward to view the prize. Cue him in advance to respond in awe as he sees it, perhaps begging you for just one more peek, etc.) Just before the worker returns to his seat, extract a promise from him—in front of all the kids—to keep it secret.

"If you'd like to win the **Mystery Prize,** just follow two rules. Number one, sit up straight; number two, no talking. At the end of Children's Church our secret agent will tell us who the winner is. That winner may be a girl, or it may be a boy. If you are the winner, the **Mystery Prize** is yours.

"Now, here's the fun part! If you win the **Mystery Prize,** you may open the bag and show it to everyone in Children's Church, or you may keep it a secret! If you choose to keep it a secret, we'll staple the bag closed, and everyone else will wonder what the **Mystery Prize** was. They'll wonder for the rest of their lives! Besides you, Mr. Jenkins and I will be the only ones in the whole world that know! And we won't tell!

"Start working for the **Mystery Prize** right now, and at the close of church today we'll find out who the winner is."

Other behavior awards such as **Let's Make a Deal** are most effective when used for several weeks running, but **Mystery Prize** should be used only occasionally, one Sunday at a time.

(g) RING TOSS, BEAN BAG TOSS, etc. Many of the carnival-type games make excellent behavior award games. Simply have the winning students play the game at the end of Children's Church, with various scores earning different prizes.

A catalog of the various carnival games is available from: U.S. Toy Company, 1227 East 119th Street, Grandview, Missouri 64030-1117 (1-800-255-6124).

(h) BONUS PRIZE. Here's one final idea for the behavior award. Before class, mark one of several prizes with a special mark in a place where the students will not notice it. At the conclusion of Children's Church, select the best-behaved students and present the prizes from which they are to choose. The student who chooses the marked prize receives the bonus prize: a larger, more expensive item.

I trust that these behavior award ideas will be fun for you and your Children's Church students. Each of the ideas I've just shared has worked with "my kids" and has helped make Children's Church fun and exciting. The key to motivating the kids to try for the behavior award is to use **VARIETY**. Play **Let's Make a Deal** for four or five Sundays, then try **The Mad Dash** for three or four weeks. Use the **Balloon Bust Board** for a few Sundays, then move on to another idea. As with the other parts of your Children's Church program, you want **VARIETY** in your behavior awards.

I used to work in a large Junior Church with several hundred juniors. Every Sunday, our Junior Church director gave away twelve one-liter bottles of Coke—week after week, twelve bottles of Coke; month after month, twelve bottles of Coke. Needless to say, the majority of the kids were not at all motivated to try to win the behavior award. It was the same old thing every Sunday—twelve one-liter bottles of Coke. Use **VARIETY!**

10. Develop Relationships With the Students

It's not enough to walk into Children's Church on Sunday morning, conduct a program for the kids, then walk away. That's not really a ministry.

You need to get to know the children to whom you minister, and they need to get to know you. Develop a special relationship with each child. The only way to do this is to spend time with them.

Visit regularly in the homes of your students. Get to know the child and his family. Plan regular outings for your Children's Church. Invite the kids over to your home for meals and activities. When you have fun with your students outside the classroom, you form important bonds with them. Your ministry will be greatly enhanced.

Some of my students' favorite outings were outdoor activities. Hayrides, cave trips and canoeing were at the top of the list! We planned a Children's Church outing every month, and our ministry to the children thrived. I kept our workers busy, but they (and the kids) loved every minute of it!

Do you have an especially difficult student (or students)? Are you trying to minister to some kids that are real troublemakers in class and seem determined to create a disturbance every time they come? It's easy to resent kids like this, and sometimes hard to love them!

Pray for these kids, and then plan on spending extra time with them. Take them visiting with you; let them help you with bulletin boards and other class projects; invite them out to McDonald's! (Always be sure to get parental permission, and have at least two children with you at all times so there is never any suspicion of wrong motives. In today's society, it's always best to have another adult along.)

Even the most difficult children can be won by love. I've seen it happen time after time! It may take awhile, but once you win the heart of a "problem kid," you've got a friend for life! If you'll take the time, kids like this can become the greatest joys of your entire ministry.

Classroom control is a must as we teach children the eternal truths of God's Word. With a lot of prayer, some work and preparation and a little bit of creativity, you can plan on having an orderly, well-disciplined class! Love those kids, pray for them and work on developing the most exciting, most interesting Children's Church they have ever seen. The results will be worth it.

Maintaining Good Discipline

1. Pray.

2. Be well-prepared.

3. Teach with enthusiasm!

4. Make maximum use of visual aids.

5. Practice good eye contact.

6. Seat your workers among the students.

7. Consider rearranging your classroom.

8. Expect good behavior.

9. Use behavior awards.
   a. Let's Make a Deal
   b. The Price Is Right
   c. Balloon Bust Board
   d. The Mad Dash
   e. King and Queen
   f. The Mystery Prize
   g. Carnival Games
   h. Bonus Prize

10. Develop relationships with the students.

Why do students misbehave?

Many times discipline problems occur in Children's Church because the teacher is unprepared or the teaching hour is boring. But some students "act up" even during a well-planned, quality program. Below is a list of common causes:

1. Need for attention
2. Need for sense of belonging
3. Rebellion because of rejection
4. Lack of self-worth or self-confidence
5. Spiritual problems
6. Peer group pressures
7. Challenge to authority
8. Undesirable home conditions:
   a. Divorce
   b. No rules or discipline
   c. Favoritism
   d. Overly harsh discipline
   e. Abuse—physical, verbal or sexual

The teacher who desires to reach every student for Christ will visit in the home and get to know the background of each student in order to address and meet the needs of each.

Checking Up on Discipline

YES NO

___ ___ 1. Are my students orderly and attentive during Children's Church?

___ ___ 2. Am I cheerful and friendly to my students?

___ ___ 3. Do I actually enjoy being with them?

___ ___ 4. Do I pray for each of my students during the week?

___ ___ 5. Do I pray during class, asking God to settle all of my students and focus their attention on the lesson?

___ ___ 6. Am I so well-prepared that the program flows smoothly and holds the attention of the students?

___ ___ 7. Am I excited about teaching?

___ ___ 8. Do I teach with enthusiasm?

___ ___ 9. Do I make use of a VARIETY of visual aids?

___ ___ 10. Do I use my visual aids smoothly and efficiently?

___ ___ 11. Do I practice good eye contact with my students?

___ ___ 12. Does my classroom create a good learning environment?

___ ___ 13. Do my workers sit among the students?

___ ___ 14. Are they alert to discipline problems around them?

Checking Up on Discipline, Cont.

YES NO

__ __ 15. Do they handle problems quietly and discreetly?

__ __ 16. Do my workers pray for the students?

__ __ 17. Do we expect good behavior during class?

__ __ 18. If a student is unruly or disruptive, do we deal with the student privately, rather than embarrassing him/her in class?

__ __ 19. Do I love the unruly students, rather than resenting them?

__ __ 20. If I momentarily lose the attention of my students during the lesson, do I know how to regain it by changing pace, introducing a visual aid, or telling a story?

__ __ 21. Do I make good use of behavior awards?

__ __ 22. Do I use a VARIETY of awards from week to week?

__ __ 23. Are my workers completely impartial in selecting the winning students?

__ __ 24. Does each student see Children's Church as "my class" instead of "my teacher's class"?

Ask Andy!

Dear Andy,

We have an outstanding Junior Church program, some fantastic workers and some really awesome kids. I think working in Junior Church is the neatest ministry there is.

Our problem is one of our "bus kids," a boy I'll call Jason. This one kid can turn the Junior Church service upside down all by himself! He starts fights, cusses and does everything he can to create disturbances during the service. In fact, some of our church families are refusing to let their kids come to Junior Church now, just because of Jason! And last week he actually punched one of our workers when she tried to correct him!

Most of the workers want to kick Jason out of Junior Church, so we don't lose any other kids because of him. Sometimes, I think they're right, and sometimes I think we need to give Jason another chance.

What do you say?

Chuck Roast

Dear Chuck,

You're probably right—unless something is done about the situation, you are going to lose kids because of Jason. But I beg you: don't "kick Jason out" of Junior Church except as a final, desperate measure.

One of the men in Junior Church needs to take Jason on as a special "project." (Perhaps that person could be you.) Start by visiting in Jason's home. I can almost guarantee that you're going to find an abusive situation. Once you see his homelife, I think you'll begin to understand where he's coming from.

And then, set out to win Jason's heart. Take him with you on visitation, on hikes or fishing trips, to McDonald's or Burger King. Just be a friend to him! (A word of caution: in today's society, it's best if you always have two kids with you so your motives are never under suspicion.)

It will take some time, and perhaps a little patience, but if you really care, you can win his heart! I've seen it happen with some of our worst troublemakers. And believe me, the results are worth the effort.

For the children,

Andy

Dear Andy,

We don't really have discipline problems with our kids in Children's Church. Our problem is with one of the church leaders—the head usher.

This guy waits until the middle of our service, then pops in and takes a head count! He actually walks about halfway down the center aisle as he takes his count. It only takes a minute or two, but needless to say, it's a real distraction.

We've tried to talk with him about it, but he says he's only doing his job.

Any suggestions?

Justin Case

Dear Justin,

This can be a touchy one. You don't want to develop this into a power play, but you can't let this distraction go unchecked, either.

Next Sunday, take an accurate head count well before the time that the usher usually comes in. Write the count on a slip of paper, then post a worker outside the door with it. This worker should meet the usher and explain diplomatically but firmly that the count has been taken, and henceforth will always be posted outside the door. And always be sure that the count is posted when it needs to be.

Andy

Dear Andy,

Do you think it's right to reward the good kids in Children's Church? Isn't that bribing them? And shouldn't they be good just because they're in the house of the Lord?

Manda Lynn

Dear Manda Lynn,

How many adults do you know who always do what's right, just because it's right? Most of us need some extra motivation.

If the Lord plans to give us a reward for giving a child a cup of cold water in His name, don't you think it's right for us to give rewards to children who do well? I believe so.

Thanks for writing.

For the children,

Andy

Dear Andy,

We have a fourth-grade girl in our Children's Church who is nothing but trouble. Whenever a worker corrects her, she screams, "Don't touch me! My mom will sue you!" To be honest, we're not really sure what to do with her, and she pretty much does whatever she wants.

This girl rides the bus, and I don't know her parents, but is it possible that her mom could cause trouble for our church if we correct her?

Ella Vader

Dear Ella,

Be careful—a kid with an "attitude" can create real problems for your ministry.

I would visit this girl's home, ASAP. Talk with her parent(s), and explain that you are grateful for the opportunity to minister to the child, but that you are having discipline problems.

Ask God to give you discernment as you talk with the parents. If the parents are behind you, they'll probably take care of the problem for you. If, however, you sense that the parents are hostile toward you and the church, you might be wise to drop that child from your bus route.

You cannot minister to a child whom you cannot correct, and there are families that would jump at the chance to create trouble for your church. Pray for wisdom.

For the kids,

Andy

Dear Andy,

When our Primaries and Juniors come out of Sunday School, it's as if World War III just broke loose! The kids scatter everywhere—some in the rest rooms, some to the drinking fountain, and some even make it outside to the playground! By the time we get them all rounded up and start Children's Church, you might as well forget it. We get off to a bad start every week.

Any suggestions?

Candy Kaine

Dear Candy,

You're not alone! Many Children's Churches get off to the same chaotic start every Sunday, but it doesn't have to be that way.

Call a meeting of all the Primary and Junior Sunday school teachers, and ask them to march their classes to

49

the Children's Church room at dismissal time. Assure them that you and your staff will be ready to take charge of the kids at that point.

Seat the kids as they enter the room. Inform them that they are allowed to talk quietly, then dismiss those who need to take a rest-room break, but only two or three at a time. As soon as the rest-room needs are taken care of, start your program with a fun opener.

An orderly start helps the rest of the hour tremendously! Get off to a rough start, and you'll probably have a rough finish.

For the kids,

4.
PRESENTING THE BIBLE LESSON

In today's world, everything has to be instant. We want everything prepared for us, and we want it *now*. No one seems to want to expend any effort to accomplish any task, no matter how worthwhile. Grandma's melt-in-your-mouth chocolate cake lovingly made from scratch has been replaced with a boxed mix that even a first grader can dump together. Not quite the same as Grandma's, but much, much easier!

Even this isn't fast enough. Now the mix-together-pop-in-the-oven cake mix is being replaced by an even faster culinary phenomenon, the microwave cake! This tasteless marvel can be prepared in less time than it takes to read the directions.

For those who don't even have the time for the microwave cake, there's always the ready-made cake available at the supermarket bakery. The only effort required is to pick up this plastic-shrouded dessert and plop it on the checkout stand. It's a far cry from Grandma's cake, but oh, so convenient!

Many Children's Church teachers want the same ease and convenience in their teaching of God's Word. They saunter into the local Christian bookstore, select the Children's Church kit with the flashiest packaging, and figure that most of the work is done! Instead of "just add water," the directions could read "just add a voice"! Is this teaching?

The Bible lesson should:
1. Catch the attention.
2. Hold the interest.
3. Create desire.
4. Inspire action.

There are some good teaching materials available, but many of the offerings have very little Bible content. Many publishers are striving to produce a "generic" teaching product, material that will sell to everyone but teach nothing. A pastor friend of mine recently received a phone call from a sales rep attempting to push a Children's Church curriculum. The pleasant female voice on the line assured him that the material did not "teach doctrine"!

Then why use any teaching materials? Well, they can be a valuable source of ideas, suggestions, teaching hints and visual aids. A quality, Bible-based curriculum, whether for Sunday school or Children's Church, is written by professionals who understand their age groups and know the best methods for teaching them. They are writers, able to put on paper the help that we as teachers need. They can help us with the how-to of working with our kids.

Cindy sez: "When Mr. Titus teaches, the Bible lesson is my favorite part of Junior Church!"

So read the lesson materials and research the curriculums, gleaning from them any useful methods and ideas; but don't get locked into teaching the lesson just the way they present it. Remember, the materials were written by "experts," but these are people who have never met *your* Juniors. They may understand the basic needs of Primaries, but they've never spent an hour with one of *your* Primaries.

If you use a teaching curriculum, use it as the teaching tool for which it was intended. Consider the teaching suggestions in the light of your class. Adapt the concepts to meet the needs of your students. Study the Scriptures and seek God's guidance as to how to present the lesson to your Children's Church.

Sometimes it's better yet to prepare your own lessons, structuring them to meet your students' needs.

Where does the Bible lesson start? It actually starts with the spiritual needs of your pupils. As we stated earlier, an effective teacher spends time with the children he or she teaches, visiting in the homes, planning activities and outings together, and always watching, listening, observing.

Get to know your students. Only by knowing the needs of the pupils in your particular class and by understanding their backgrounds can you hope to minister to them as individuals. With the needs of the students carefully taken into consideration, you are ready to select a teaching aim.

The Bible lesson should meet the students' needs.

There are two basic types of Bible lessons. The main thrust of the **evangelistic lesson** is salvation, a clear presentation of the Gospel. This type of lesson would include a concise presentation of the plan of salvation and conclude with a salvation invitation.

The second type of lesson is for **Christian growth**, and the main emphasis would be on teaching and challenging the believers to live for Christ. The objective of the Christian growth lessons is the instruction of young believers, equipping them to live their faith. Perhaps the message of salvation is included briefly in these lessons, but that is not their primary objective.

Know your students. If the Children's Church is made up entirely of professing Christians, the alert teacher will prepare lessons that challenge them to real Christian living and witnessing. If many in the class have not received Christ, an emphasis needs to be placed on salvation. Again, the Bible lesson should meet the spiritual needs of the students.

The lesson must be planned.

Fourteen years ago, a friend from church helped me build the house in which my family and I now live. It was quite a project, requiring dawn-to-dusk work for nearly three months. I had never built an entire house before, and I really had no idea just how much work was involved.

Before we even staked out the plot for the bulldozer to begin the excavation work, I knew almost exactly how the finished house would look. We had a blueprint. Every closet, every window, every electrical outlet was laid out on paper before we even picked up a hammer. I had hired an architect to draw plans for my house, and as we built, we simply followed the plan.

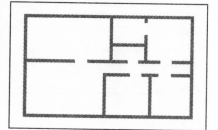

It's the same with teaching. Your Children's Church lesson must be planned in advance so the resulting structure will be attractive and lasting. Successful teaching depends on proper planning.

My Lesson Plan

Date:_____

Scripture Text:_____

Teaching Aim: [Brief, clear, specific + achievable]

Materials Needed for Lesson:

_____
_____
_____
_____
_____
_____

TEACHING PROCEDURE:

Opening (interest gainer):_____

_____

Main points in the Bible story:

_____
_____
_____
_____

Points of application:

_____
_____
_____

Closing:

_____
_____

Results:_____

_____

See page 64 for a sample

How foolish is the builder who would attempt to erect a building without a plan! And yet many Children's Church teachers attempt it every Sunday.

A lesson plan is a step-by-step arrangement of the methods and materials that the teacher will use to help the students learn. Because each lesson and class are different, the teacher must prepare a different plan for each lesson. And because each teacher is different, it is always best if the teacher himself draws up the lesson plan.

The lesson plan describes the following: (1) a teaching objective or aim; (2) the materials needed; (3) a plan of presentation, usually a detailed outline or step-by-step procedure including the methods that will be employed; and (4) a description of the planned opening and closing, including the points of application.

A well-prepared lesson plan results in quality teaching; a poorly prepared plan or no plan at all is a sure-fire formula for ineffective teaching. The very first step toward a quality lesson is a quality lesson plan!

The lesson must have a specific aim.

As you study the lesson, write out a specific teaching aim. As Findley Edge tells us in his excellent book, *Teaching for Results*, our teaching aim must be brief enough to be remembered, clear enough to be written down, and specific enough to be achieved. The entire Children's Church program revolves around the Bible lesson, while the Bible lesson revolves around one central teaching aim.

The lesson aim is the target toward which the teacher shoots with the Bible lesson. It is the objective, the goal, the purpose that the teacher hopes to accomplish with the lesson. Notice the lesson aim on the sample lesson plan for Mark 2:1–12 (page 64)—"To help the child find ways in which he can witness for Jesus."

Every part of the lesson—the opening, the Bible story, the application, the visuals, the closing—should point toward this one aim. The lesson accomplishes its purpose because the teaching aim ties the whole lesson together, giving unity and direction.

Once you have selected your teaching aim, build the lesson around it. The **lesson opening** should introduce the idea or concept to your

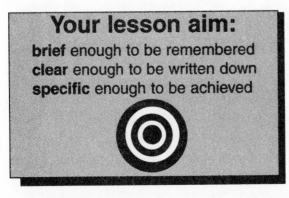

Your lesson aim:
brief enough to be remembered
clear enough to be written down
specific enough to be achieved

students, perhaps with a short story or vivid illustration.

The **Bible story** illustrates and explains the teaching aim; the **application** and **closing** help drive it home to the hearts of the students. A concise, clear, specific teaching aim is essential to lesson preparation.

It's also essential that you communicate your lesson aim to the workers who will have a part in the Children's Church service. Your song leader should know your aim well in advance so he or she can choose appropriate songs. The song service should teach the same concept as the lesson!

Convey your teaching aim to your puppeteers early enough for them to select and practice an appropriate puppet skit. How embarrassing for a puppet troupe to present a program on *honesty*, then learn that you are teaching on *witnessing*! The person who is to present the missionary story will appreciate the information also so she can select the story that reinforces your theme or work the theme into the story she has chosen.

Perhaps the greatest fault of the average teacher in lesson preparation is the failure to build the lesson around a clear, concise, specific teaching aim. Don't make this same mistake. Build your entire program around your teaching aim, with the various aspects complementing each other.

The lesson must be on the students' level.

Learn to tailor your illustrations to the interests of your students. If you are aware that some of your students live, sleep and eat baseball, an occasional illustration from that sport will be a hit with them. Is *honesty* the theme of today's lesson? A story involving corporate fraud and insider trading will have far less impact than an interesting story about cheating in a BMX race. The lesson should meet the students where they live.

An alert teacher would not open the lesson from Mark 2 with a stirring illustration of a fiery evangelist reaching the masses with the Gospel. Rather, she would perhaps share a story of a third-grade girl who was able to lead three friends to Christ during a slumber party. The lesson must speak to the child's heart, and to do this, it must meet him at his own level.

Consider the language and terminology used in your teaching. We teachers have heard Bible words so often that we sometimes forget how foreign they can be to a child. Do your students know the meaning of the word *justification*? If not, clearly define the term when you use it, or perhaps better yet, use the simple phrase "when God forgives us." Your children may not know the word *redeem*, but they do understand "buy back."

> And so, children, the ultimate result of the vicarious atonement is our redemption and justification!

Use terms that mean what they say and say what they mean. Remember that children, especially younger ones, think literally. Have you ever stopped to imagine the mental image a first grader receives when we speak of being "on fire for God"? Why urge students to "give your heart to Jesus" when we really mean "ask Jesus to save you from sin"? Instead of giving an invitation for your pupils to "ask Jesus into your heart," why not invite them to "receive Jesus as your Saviour"? The words we use in teaching children *must* say what they mean and mean what they say.

Again, it's vital for the teacher to know the students and to be aware of their backgrounds. Children who have been in church all of their lives will have a far more extensive biblical vocabulary than the child who rides the bus for his very first visit to church.

As you prepare the Children's Church lesson, examine and evaluate the terms and expressions you will use. Are there any words that will be unfamiliar or vague to your students? Plan to drop them, substituting simpler, more familiar terms. Are there any unfamiliar words in the Bible passage? Look them up in a Bible dictionary, then rehearse a simple definition to explain them to your students. The pupil *must* understand the lesson if he is to benefit from it.

Checking our terminology

Which of these terms mean what they say and say what they mean? Which use abstract or figurative language?

"Give your heart to Jesus"	"Salvation"	"Receive Jesus as Saviour"
"On fire for God"	"Omnipotent"	"Eternal life"
"Omniscient"	"All-powerful"	"Omnipresent"
"All-knowing"		"Always-present"
"Faith"	"Trusting God"	"Ask Jesus into your heart"
"The gift of God"	"Your all on the altar"	"Believe"
"Everlasting life"	"Repent"	"Ask Jesus to save you"

Which would be suitable for a class of Primaries and Juniors? Which would not? Which would need explanation? Which are Bible terms?

The lesson should usually be built around a Bible story.

Many teachers, especially those who work with adults, dismiss storytelling as a frivolous teaching method. They fail to see that storytelling is a most effective teaching method for any age group, and they forget that it was the favorite method of the Master Teacher, the Lord Jesus!

Storytelling is one of the most powerful teaching methods known to man. A good story grabs the child's attention, conveys truth in an enjoyable, interesting way, and makes a lasting impression upon his heart. A good story can involve the listener emotionally, change his or her attitude, and move him or her to action. A good story captivates the student and invites him to become a part of the action. If you learn only one method of teaching, learn the

> "A good story grabs the child's attention, conveys truth in an enjoyable, interesting way, and makes a lasting impression upon his heart."

Storytelling

Sources of stories or illustrations:
1. **The Bible**
2. **Jesus' sources**
   (a) **Farm life**
   (b) **Homelife**
   (c) **Political life**
   (d) **Business life**
3. **Personal experience**
   (a) **Childhood**
   (b) **Work**
   (c) **Family**
4. **Current events**
5. **Nature**
6. **Sermons and speeches**
7. **Other teachers**
8. **Teachers' helps**
9. **Books of stories and illustrations**

Qualities of a good story:
1. **Relevant**
   (a) **To the lesson**
   (b) **To the life experience of the students**
2. **Interesting**
3. **Accurate**
4. **Appropriate length**
5. **Clear**
6. **Fresh**

59

art of storytelling. It's powerful!

Teaching materials abound with modern stories, some of them visualized, some not. Some are true stories, some are fiction, and sometimes it's hard to tell which are real and which are not.

Why not find your teaching stories in the greatest story resource of all times, the Bible? When you build your lesson around a Bible story, you know that it's a true story, and you know that the details are accu-

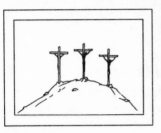

rate. When you teach a Bible story, you're not only sharing a good illustration of truth but continuing to acquaint your students with God's Word. God has promised to bless His Word. Bible stories are far more effective than the "Barney's Barrel" type story.

An alert teacher may use a modern-day story as an opener, perhaps even an incident from her own experience—if the students will relate to it—but then she will proceed to use a Bible story as the main body of the lesson.

Each point of truth, each facet of application, can be presented through the vehicle of the Bible story. Perhaps a short, modern-day story is told to conclude the lesson and illustrate the application, but the Bible story provides the primary structure upon which the lesson is assembled.

An effective Bible lesson will actually involve a VARIETY of methods. In addition to the storytelling, the alert teacher will sometimes make use of lecture, discussion, question and answer, even role-playing! Methods such as storytelling and lecture which involve teacher-to-student communication are most effective when used in combination with student-to-teacher methods such as question and answer.

As you prepare your lesson plan, prayerfully select the method or methods which will most naturally convey your lesson aim.

The lesson should be visualized.

If you're not convinced that visual aids are essential to your teaching, try this simple experiment. Turn your television so that the screen faces the wall, then "watch" your favorite program or the evening news with the audio alone! Quite a difference, isn't there? Do you get the feeling that something's missing?

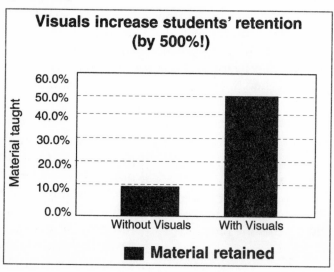

Visuals greatly enhance the effectiveness of your teaching. *A visual, properly used, will grab the student's attention, help him understand the lesson, and cause him to remember it.* Why would anyone teach without them?

As with other parts of the Children's Church ministry, visuals are most effective when there is VARIETY. Sorry, there's that word again. So many teachers get comfortable with just one or two methods of

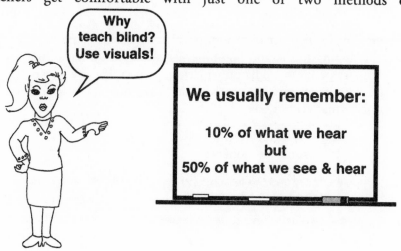

visualization. After a time, an over-used visual aid becomes "invisible" and loses its impact and effectiveness.

As a Junior High student, I attended a church where the pastor used the overhead projector in his messages. He had the projector mounted beside the pulpit and flipped it on at various points during the sermon. The problem was that he used it for every single service! In two years of attendance at that church, I never heard a message that didn't include the overhead projector!

Joey sez:

"I like it when Miss Perry teaches! She uses a lot of pictures and stuff. That helps me understand, and it helps me remember!"

Take a glance at the list of various visual aids on the next page. Scan through the list, placing a check mark in the box beside any visual that you regularly use. Now, go through the list again, paying attention to the visuals with no check marks. Why not take a challenge—learn to use the visuals that are new to you! The VARIETY will greatly enhance your teaching ministry, and the challenge of something new can bring freshness to your own experience.

Visuals don't have to be elaborate to be effective. Last year I saw a multi-media presentation that incorporated more than a dozen projectors, three giant screens, and an elaborate sound system. The presentation was powerful. At the close of the program I walked out of the auditorium feeling almost overwhelmed; but that one presentation cost $135,000 to prepare! The brilliant images on the screens dissolving so perfectly in sync with the stirring music and booming narration would have little impact on a Primary or Junior. The presentation, powerful as it was, would even begin to lose its effectiveness with adults if the message was presented in the same format every week.

Visual aids:
catch the student's attention, help him to understand the lesson, and cause him to remember it!

How many different VISUAL AIDS have you used?

☐ Flashcards	☐ Sand Table
☐ Objects	☐ Blacklight Scene
☐ Charts & Graphs	☐ Sketchboard
☐ Maps	☐ Flip Charts
☐ Flannelgraph	☐ Posters
☐ Overhead Projector	☐ Bulletin Boards
☐ Chalkboard	☐ Pictures
☐ Marker Board	☐ Models
☐ Video	☐ Puppets
☐ Movie Projector	☐ Role Play
☐ Filmstrip Projector	☐ Costumes
☐ Slide Projector	☐ Handouts

Check the list for any visuals that you have never used, then learn to use them to enhance your Junior Church!

My Lesson Plan

Date: 6-4-96

Scripture Text: Mark 2:1–12

Teaching Aim: To help the child find ways in which he can witness for Jesus

Materials Needed for Lesson:
Lesson #7–"Four Men Tear Up a Roof" (16 Figures)
Model house, 5 chenille figures
Marker board, 2 markers
Flannel board
Word cards (3)
100 gospel tracts

TEACHING PROCEDURE:

Opening (interest gainer): Story–"The Slumber Party"
(3rd-grade girl witnesses)

Main points in the Bible story:
1. Care—Friends become concerned.
2. Do something—Friends bring man.
3. Don't give up!—Friends go to roof to
   gain access.

See page 67 for transition idea

Points of application:
1. People need Jesus.
2. Each of us can be a witness.
3. List ways (children's ideas)

Closing:
Challenge to give tracts
Story of Jessica

Results:_____

Sometimes the simplest visuals are the most effective. And VARI-ETY increases their impact.

The teacher preparing the message from Mark 2 is planning to use flannelgraph to visualize the Bible story. She also has some chenille wire figures and a 3-D posterboard house with a trapdoor in the roof for the part about lowering the sick man through the roof, and she'll use these in a tabletop display. She prepared some first-class word cards on bright card stock (using her computer) for the lesson application, and she also has her dry erase board ready for the discussion part of the application.

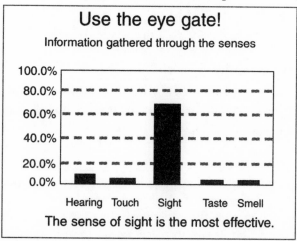

Her visuals are simple, to be sure, but they're going to be effective! Why? They're appropriate and call attention to the lesson rather than to themselves. They're well-planned, and the lesson will flow smoothly as she uses them in her presentation. And there's VARIETY—several different visuals in just one lesson. What more could you ask for?

Objects can become the simplest yet most effective visual aids. Are you planning a message on the Bible, the "sword of the Spirit"? Why not visualize it in part with a plastic sword? If one is not available, make a large sword from cardboard and paint it with silver spray paint!

A lesson on the feeding of the five thousand could be effectively visualized with a basket of biscuits and frozen fish fillets. Your lesson on the Passover will be much more interesting if during the story you paint the lintel and doorposts of the classroom door with an oleander branch dipped in catsup. Candles, coins, bread, shoes, hammers, water and clothing can all become powerful additions to your lesson. Simple objects are effective visuals.

A dry erase board can be a very inexpensive way to visualize. Buy a 4' x 8' sheet of Marlite (white board) at any building supply house. Have them cut the sheet into 27" x 36" pieces, saving the leftover pieces. This will give you three marker boards, which you can trim out with duct tape. Cut the scraps into 12" x 16" rectangles, trim the edges with duct tape; now you have portable erase boards known as "walkie-talkie" boards.

The dry erase markers come in at least eight different colors and can be wiped from the surface with a dry tissue (or even a bare hand). Use the erase board to list key words or phrases, draw diagrams, even illustrate the story with stick figures.

I was in the audience when a lecturer showed a crowd of teachers how to draw a horse and chariot on the marker board. He sketched the chariot at the extreme edge of the board with the horse out of the picture! He got a good laugh, but he also demonstrated how simple visuals can be.

Flannelgraph can be beautiful and effective. Staple your background scenes to 27" x 36" sheets of cardboard (large boxes are available at furniture stores), then trim the edges with duct tape. Your scenes can now be changed with figures still in place, rather than flipping them over the top of the easel and dropping the figures.

Tired of flannelgraph—or more importantly, are your students tired of it? Cut various colors of pastel-colored posterboard into 12" x 16" sheets, then rubber cement the flannelgraph figures for next Sunday's lesson to the posterboard to make flashcards. Or use a photocopier to reduce the flannelgraph figures onto construction paper, cut them out, and use them to visualize the story in silhouette on the overhead projector!

This past August, I was speaking to a crowd of several hundred Juniors at a Christian camp in North Carolina. Wednesday morning I realized that I had left my overhead transparencies for that day's message, the ten lepers, at a church three hours away. I nearly panicked, but the Lord gave me a simple idea.

A quarter, placed on the projector, represented Jesus for the story, and ten nickels became the ten lepers. I slid the ten nickels toward the quarter as the lepers approached Jesus to be healed. Jesus sent the ten lepers away—the nickels retreated to the opposite side of the projector stage—but one man came back to thank Jesus. As I slid the one lone nickel back toward the quarter, leaving the other nine nickels at the opposite side, I found myself thinking, *This is almost as effective as my transparencies would have been!*

Visual aids are effective. They ought to look nice, but they need not always be elaborate. As you teach the lesson, visuals catch the students' attention, help them understand and cause them to remember. Why should we ever teach without them?

The lesson must be applied.

As the lesson progresses, the teacher must assist the pupils in applying the biblical truth to their own lives. She must help them become "doers of the word, and not hearers only." The lesson must be integrated into the very fabric of the students' everyday lives.

The Children's Church teacher might draw the application of the lesson from Mark 2 in this way:

"And so, the sick man was healed and forgiven, because he came to Jesus. The greatest need in his life was to see Jesus. He could not walk, but his four friends cared enough to bring him.

"Every one of you knows someone who needs the Lord, someone who has never received Him as Saviour. Perhaps it is a relative, a neighbor, a friend. You could be the one to help bring that person to Jesus!

"Now, stop and think. If you know someone who is not saved, what could you do to be a witness to that person, to help bring him or her to Jesus?"

At this point, the teacher calls on various students to offer ideas, then writes their suggestions on the marker board. The lesson becomes intensely personal because each child suddenly sees how the Bible story applies to his or her own life situation.

The teacher may then drive the application home just a bit further by offering a stack of gospel tracts. "As you leave church today, there will be gospel tracts by the door. These are papers that tell about Jesus and how to receive Him as Saviour.

"If you would like to give a tract to a friend who needs the Lord, why not take one as you leave church in a few minutes? Ask God to use you to take the Good News to your friend."

The teacher has made the lesson personal, and the students have no trouble applying it to their own lives. She has also followed through with a simple way for the students actually to put the lesson into practice, a tangible way to be a witness—giving out a simple gospel tract. The students have heard the lesson; now they actually have the opportunity to act upon it.

 Do you remember how Jesus closed the "Sermon on the Mount"? He closed with a very brief account of the houses built on the sand and on the rock, then gave the admonition to do "these sayings of mine." We should close our Children's Church lessons in a similar fashion.

You've been teaching one or both of two classes of students: those who do not know the Saviour and need to be invited to receive Him and those who do know Him and need to be encouraged or challenged to obey Him fully. Your closing should open the door for both groups to respond to God's call. We'll discuss the invitation in Chapter 6.

The Bible lesson is by far the most important element in the Children's Church program. It requires more preparation, prayer, work and time than any other part of the service. We dare not do a second-rate job in this vital area of our ministry to the children. We dare not give less than our best. Souls are at stake.

The Bible lesson

...should meet students' needs.

...must be carefully planned.

...must have a specific aim.

...must be on the students' level.

...should present a Bible story.

...should be visualized.

...must be applied.

Integrating Your Teaching Aim

Every component of the Junior Church program should reinforce the teaching aim of the Bible lesson.

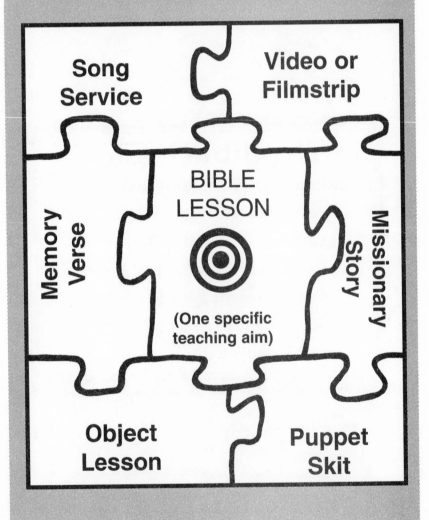

Evaluating My Bible Lessons

YES   NO

__ __   **1. Do I begin lesson preparation early in the week?**

__ __   **2. Do I spend a minimum of 2 hours in lesson preparation?**

__ __   **3. Do I see the Bible lesson as being the most important part of the entire program?**

__ __   **4. Do I put more work, preparation, and prayer into the lesson than any other aspect of the program?**

__ __   **5. Do I study the Bible passage before studying any lesson manual?**

__ __   **6. Do my lessons meet the students' spiritual needs?**

__ __   **7. Do I build each lesson around a carefully chosen teaching aim?**

__ __   **8. Are my teaching aims clear, brief and specific?**

__ __   **9. Are my lessons on the students' level?**

__ __ **10. Do I use terminology that is familiar and meaningful to my students?**

__ __ **11. Are my illustrations appropriate to my students' age level and interests?**

and next page

71

Evaluating My Bible Lessons, Cont.

YES   NO

___ ___12.   Do I usually build the lesson around a Bible story?

___ ___13.   Have I developed my skills as a storyteller?

___ ___14.   Do I visualize each lesson?

___ ___15.   Do I visualize the application, as well as the Bible story?

___ ___16.   Are my visual aids attractive?

___ ___17.   Are they appropriate to the lesson?

___ ___18.   Do my visuals call attention to the lesson, rather than to themselves?

___ ___19.   Do I use a VARIETY of visual aids, rather than locking into one or two favorites to the point of overuse?

___ ___20.   Do I know how to apply the lesson to the lives of the pupils?

___ ___21.   Do I find tangible ways for my students to put the truths of the lesson into practice?

___ ___22.   Are my lessons interesting and challenging?

Ask Andy!

Dear Andy,

In our church we've always had a hard time coming up with workers for Children's Church. Who in their right minds want to be stuck with a bunch of noisy kids, when they could be enjoying the morning service?

But we've finally settled on a workable solution: we have a rotating Children's Church staff!

Two couples take the first service in the month, another two couples the second Sunday, etc. Each team serves only one Sunday a month, then they have the other three Sundays off. It has solved a lot of problems.

Just thought I'd share our idea with you.

Iona Bank

Dear Iona,

At first glance, yours seems like an ideal solution to an age-old problem. With your system, no one has to put out more than once a month, and so there's no real need for total commitment to the Children's Church ministry.

But suppose we applied the same system to the entire church ministry. Let's hire four pastors! Pastor A would preach the first Sunday of the month, as well as take care of the counseling and other pastoral duties throughout that first week. On the second Sunday, Pastor B steps into the pulpit and continues serving as your pastor for the rest of the week. Pastor C comes on the third Sunday. . . .

Wait just a minute! Would that be a real ministry? Which one of these men would really be your pastor? How would any of these men establish a relationship with the congregation, or vice versa? And what happens when the church members start playing favorites—staying home on the second Sunday because Pastor B isn't as personable as Pastor D, etc.?

It's always best to have a regular staff of Children's Church teachers and workers. If you don't have enough dedicated people (folks who enjoy being with the kids, rather than resenting missing the adult service), then you need to do as Jesus suggested and pray for laborers!

Andy

Dear Andy,

We have marker boards in all of our Sunday school classes, but the markers dry up so quickly. It seems that they just last a few weeks. And at a dollar and a half per marker, that adds up! Is there one brand that lasts longer than the others?

Mark R. Board

Dear Mark,

A dry marker should last a year or two (particularly if they get Sunday only use), and most brands do. If the markers are drying out quickly, the problem is usually found in the way in which they are used and stored.

Be sure to cap the markers as soon as you are through with them, but just as important, *store them in a horizontal position!* Any dry marker will dry out quickly if left standing on end.

Most teachers are not aware of this, so you may want to pass a memo around. Happy marking!

Andy

Dear Andy,

How do we get our kids to follow through on our lessons?

We teach our hearts out, but the message seems to go in one ear and out the other. It can be pretty discouraging. Sometimes I wonder if our teaching is making any difference at all!

Any suggestions?

Sandy Shorr

Dear Sandy,

Don't give up—you're accomplishing more than you might think!

But there are ways to encourage the students to follow through on the Bible lessons and actually put our teaching into practice. I'm sure that you teach the children the importance of reading God's Word. But do you ever do anything to motivate them to do it?

How about giving out a weekly Bible-reading slip, a small sheet of paper listing the Scripture references for seven short passages? And then check the next week to see how many pupils (and workers) have done the Bible reading! After a few weeks, Bible reading will become a regular habit with some. You might even have your workers call some of the kids during the week to encourage them.

Each time you teach a lesson, apply it personally, then find some tangible way to help the students actually put the lesson into practice.

For the kids,

Andy

Dear Andy,

What's the best Bible to use with kids?

Right now we have so many different versions among our students and teachers that it's impossible to have a class read in unison. And when it comes to Scripture memory, the confusion increases.

Isn't there one Bible that most of us could settle on?
Heath Barr

Dear Heath,

This may surprise you, but in my opinion the best choice is still the King James Version. Kids don't have as much trouble with the *"thees"* and *"thous"* as we think they do, and the unfamiliar biblical terms need to be defined for kids no matter which version you're using.

Don't be afraid to suggest that your teaching staff use the King James; it's the most accurate of all the translations, contrary to some advertising you may have seen.

And while we're on the subject, let me suggest that you always teach with your Bible in hand, not some lesson manual or quarterly. Let the students see that your teaching actually comes from the Word of God. It's more important than you might think.

Andy

5.

PRESENTING THE GOSPEL
TO CHILDREN

Without a doubt the most fertile soil for the seed of the Gospel is the heart of a child. Children respond so readily to the Good News! Eighty-five percent of the people who receive Christ as Saviour do so between the ages of five and fourteen. Take the Scriptures and show a child that Jesus died for him and wants to save him, and

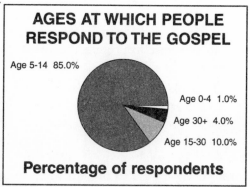

AGES AT WHICH PEOPLE RESPOND TO THE GOSPEL

Age 5-14 85.0%

Age 0-4 1.0%

Age 30+ 4.0%

Age 15-30 10.0%

Percentage of respondents

most times the natural response is, "I want to ask Him to save me. When can I do it?"

If children's hearts are the most tender and receptive to the Gospel, then it goes without saying that the heart that is not reached during the childhood years will become harder and less receptive.

We must present the message of Jesus to children! We must show our students their need of a Saviour, clearly teach the way of salvation, and gently draw them to receive Jesus and His gift of eternal life. The greatest joy in teaching is to see one of our students trust Christ as Saviour as the result of our ministry.

Even so it is not the will of your Father which is in heaven, that one of these little ones should perish.

Matthew 18:14

Salvation was designed for children. Remember the words of Jesus in Matthew 18:3? ". . . Verily I say unto you, Except ye be converted, and become as little children, ye shall not enter into the kingdom of heaven." We adults stumble over the simplicity of the Gospel, while children receive it in simple faith!

Present the Gospel at Each Service.

Plan to present the Gospel on a regular basis in your Children's Church program. Many of your Bible lessons will be geared toward the students who know the Lord and will not have a salvation emphasis.

When your program calls for a message to the saved child, at some point before the lesson, plan to present the plan of salvation. Unless you have a small group and know assuredly that every child has received Christ, it is wise to present the gospel message in one form or another in every service.

God's plan of salvation boils down to these three simple truths: (1) *I am a sinner* (Romans 3:23); (2) *Jesus died for my sins* (Romans 5:8); (3) *I must receive Jesus as my Saviour* (Romans 6:23). What a simple message, and how easily a child believes and receives it! Why complicate it? Let's consider each of these three truths for a moment, then look at the most effective ways to present them to our Children's Church students.

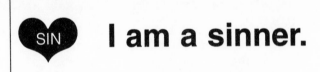

First, *I am a sinner.* Romans 3:23 tells us, "For all have sinned, and come short of the glory of God." As you present this first point in the plan of salvation, be sure to define and explain clearly what sin is. Sin is disobeying God. *Anything we do, say or think that is contrary to what God says is called sin.* When we neglect to do what God says is right, we have sinned.

As you discuss and define sin, ask your students to name some of the things kids do that are wrong. This helps to make sure that the message is personal and that each child sees himself as a sinner before God. Many times a child will readily agree that all are sinners but fail to recognize or admit his own sinfulness.

Teach the penalty for sin. Romans 6:23 tells us, "For the wages of sin is death; but the gift of God is eternal life through Jesus Christ our Lord." God's holiness demands that a penalty be paid for our sin, and that penalty is Hell. Hell is a Bible doctrine, and while we do not use it to try to scare children into a decision, it must be taught. Jesus taught more about Hell than He did about Heaven.

Jesus died for my sins.

Second, *Jesus died for my sins.* The first point of the plan is bad news, but this second point is good news! Romans 5:8 tells us, "But God commendeth [showed or proved] his love toward us, in that, while we were yet sinners, Christ died for us."

As you present the second point in the plan of salvation, which is the very heart of the Gospel, remember to stress the following: (a) Jesus is God; He was more than just a good man or a great teacher; (b) Jesus died in our place; He paid the penalty for our sins so that we may be forgiven; (c) Jesus was buried in a tomb, but came back to life three days later.

I must receive Jesus as my Saviour.

Third, *I must receive Jesus as my Saviour.* Salvation is offered as a gift, but the gift must be received. Romans 6:23 says, "For the wages of sin is death; but the gift of God is eternal life through Jesus Christ our Lord."

Lead your students to understand that Jesus died for everyone and that God offers salvation as a free gift to anyone who will receive it. Make sure that they understand that receiving Jesus by faith is a personal decision, a decision that every individual must make for himself. A person who does not receive Jesus chooses to reject Him.

As you present the Gospel to your Children's Church pupils, be sure to observe the following guidelines:

Keep the Plan of Salvation Simple.

Many times we complicate the message that God has made so simple. I once heard a man say, "God put the salvation cookie jar on the bottom shelf where the children can easily reach it. We adults have to stoop or kneel to reach it, and many times we are unwilling to do so. We try to move the cookie jar up to a higher shelf so we can be more dignified as we partake of the contents."

Joey sez:

"I asked Jesus to save me in Junior Church, and He did! I'm glad He loves kids!"

As you teach your students the truths of salvation from God's Word, explain and define your terms. Ask questions of your students as you present the Gospel, and listen carefully to their answers. Pray for discernment as you evaluate their responses. Do they understand the message, or are they simply parroting your words?

I am a sinner. SIN

Jesus died for my sins.

I must receive Jesus as my Saviour.

Be sure to use words that say what they mean and mean what they say. Remember that children think literally and do your best to avoid terms and phrases that children do not understand or that give them a wrong impression. One bit of phraseology that many children's workers use is "asking Jesus into your heart" or "giving your heart to Jesus." Do these words say what they mean and mean what they say, especially to a child who thinks literally?

Then why use this terminology? Why not talk about "asking Jesus to save you from your sins" or "receiving Jesus as your Saviour"? *Saviour, save* and *receive* are all Bible terms and easily understood. The words say what they mean and mean what they say.

Keep the message simple, and use simple terminology.

Visualize the Plan of Salvation.

One of the purposes of using visual aids is to help the students *understand* the message. What message is more important than the plan of salvation? Each time you present the gospel plan, find some way to visualize it simply. As with other parts of your teaching ministry, VARIETY adds impact to your salvation visuals. Here are some simple ways to visualize the Gospel message:

 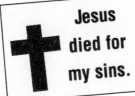 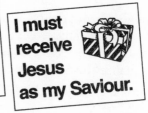

Flashcards—Stencil each of the three points of the plan on a separate flashcard, using a different color for each and placing an appropriate drawing beside the text. On the back of each card, stencil the appropriate Scripture verse that deals with that concept. For large groups, make large flashcards. (Mine are 22" x 28" with 2-inch lettering, and are visible from quite a distance.) You might even make a fourth card that reviews all three points.

For all have sinned, and come short of the glory of God. Romans 3:23

God commendeth love toward us, in ,while we were yet ners, Christ died for s. Romans 5:8

the wages of sin is h; but the gift of d is eternal life ugh Jesus Christ rd. Romans 6:23

Flannelgraph—Some Christian publishers have excellent salvation visuals prepared for the flannel board. These consist of drawings for each of the points, as well as the corresponding Scriptures. The accompanying text gives excellent tips on presenting the Gospel to children.

The Wordless Book—This is an unusual visual consisting of blank pages of various colors, each color representing one of the concepts of the gospel message. Wordless books are usually available at your local Christian bookstore.

Wordless Book Blocks—These use the same colors as the Wordless Book and simply provide VARIETY in presenting the message. The blocks nest inside one another and are revealed one by one as the teacher uses them to present the gospel plan. The same colors have been used with ribbons, gloves (each finger a different color), caterpillars, etc. An alert teacher, however, will be careful not to use a visual that is so unusual that the novelty detracts from the message.

Overhead Projector—The overhead projector is an excellent means of visualizing the plan. Each point in the gospel plan may be placed on a separate transparency, or all three may be on the same transparency using a cover sheet to reveal each point as it is presented. Be sure to visualize the Scripture verses as well. If you have access to a computer, a simple graphics program can be used to make some first-class transparencies.

Bulletin Board—Use the bulletin boards in your room to convey a message. What better message than the gospel plan? Of course you want VARIETY in your bulletin board displays, so don't leave the same arrangement up forever.

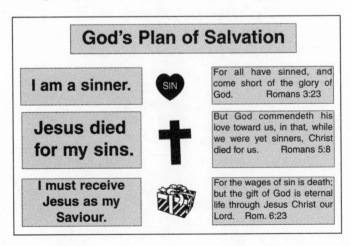

God's Plan of Salvation

I am a sinner.	SIN	For all have sinned, and come short of the glory of God. Romans 3:23
Jesus died for my sins.	✝	But God commendeth his love toward us, in that, while we were yet sinners, Christ died for us. Romans 5:8
I must receive Jesus as my Saviour.	🎁	For the wages of sin is death; but the gift of God is eternal life through Jesus Christ our Lord. Rom. 6:23

ABC—The plan of salvation can also be presented in the three basic steps using the first three letters of the alphabet. Children easily remember the concepts when the Gospel is taught in this fashion. The message is presented in this way:

A—**Admit** that you are a sinner;

B—**Believe** that Jesus died for you;

C—**Call** upon Jesus to save you.

When presenting the Gospel in the ABC format, visualize the concepts on flashcards, flannelgraph, the overhead projector, etc.

Always Use Scripture!

". . .Faith cometh by hearing, and hearing by the word of God." When you teach your students God's way of redemption, always do so from the Scriptures. Have the Bible in hand as you teach so each child realizes that it is the source of your message. When you visualize the plan of salvation, include the Bible texts in your visuals. We do not seek to *pressure* the children into getting saved, or push them into a decision; it must be the Word of God that does the persuading. Always use your Bible, and base your message on the Word.

Review, Review, Review!

Review is vital to any teaching ministry. Present the gospel plan often, visualizing in a VARIETY of ways, and always finding ways to review. Review the points of the plan during your Bible review game, including the Scripture verses. Role-play the presentation of the plan of salvation with a student or another teacher and, on occasion, let the students present the plan to each other in a role-playing exercise. This not only reviews and re-emphasizes the information in an interesting way but is also a good learning experience for the kids involved.

I must receive Jesus as my Saviour.

Pray for Your Students.

It's obvious that the best time to reach people with the Gospel is while they are young and while their hearts are still tender and receptive. As a teacher of Primaries and Juniors, you have a mission field before you each time you teach. Your students are at the prime age to be reached for the Lord. There will be no better time for them to receive Christ as Saviour than at the age they are right now. Don't let this golden opportunity slip by!

Present the Gospel carefully and prayerfully. Don't ever try to pressure a child into receiving Christ. Children will frequently "get saved" in order to please an adult or to get an adult to leave them alone, not really understanding what they are doing.

Clearly present the plan of salvation and present the child with the necessity of making a decision, but allow the child to come to a decision with the help of the Holy Spirit. Remember that is the work of the Holy Spirit. He is the One who draws people to the Saviour. As you are faithful to present the message, He will work through you to harvest young souls for His kingdom. There is no greater joy than seeing a child receive Jesus as Saviour!

The Gospel Presentation

SIN ✝ 🎁

1. Present the message in each Junior Church service.
2. Keep it simple and use understandable terminology.
3. Visualize your presentation of the Gospel.
4. Always use Scripture!
5. Review, review, review!
6. Pray for the work of the Holy Spirit in the hearts of your students.

Gospel Presentation Checklist

YES NO

___ ___ 1. Do I believe that children can receive Jesus as Saviour?

___ ___ 2. Can I give evidence from Scripture?

___ ___ 3. Do I have a burden to see my students get saved?

___ ___ 4. Do I know which of my students have received Christ and which have not?

___ ___ 5. Do I pray regularly for the salvation of my students?

___ ___ 6. Do I present the gospel plan in every service?

___ ___ 7. Do I present the plan of salvation so simply that a child can understand it?

___ ___ 8. Do I use simple Bible words, avoiding abstract or confusing terminology?

___ ___ 9. Do I use visual aids as I present the Gospel?

___ ___ 10. Are my visuals appropriate, explaining and clarifying concepts rather than confusing them?

___ ___ 11. Do I always use Scripture to present the Gospel?

___ ___ 12. Do I review the plan frequently?

Ask Andy!

Dear Andy,

At what age do kids really understand the Gospel? Can a young child actually receive Christ as Saviour and really mean it? I've seen teachers put pressure on kids to get saved, and I'm not sure it's wise.

Rusty Fender

Dear Rusty,

It's never wise to pressure any child into making a decision to receive Christ. The Holy Spirit needs to be allowed to work in the child's heart; He's the One who draws people to the Saviour.

As to your question regarding the age at which a child can understand the Gospel—it varies. Some kids are actually ready to receive Christ at age four or five; others are not ready until several years later. A child who is reared in a Christian home and hears the Scriptures on a regular basis will almost always be ready long before a child from a non-Christian home.

Again, let me emphasize the fact that no child should ever be "pushed" into a decision. Present the Gospel faithfully and allow God to work in that child's heart.

Andy

Dear Andy,

We have a kid in our Children's Church who is a holy terror!

In all my years of teaching, I've never seen a kid like this. I'm sure he's headed straight for prison.

Well, two weeks ago Scott got saved. He actually walked forward and talked with a worker after church. End of problem, right? Wrong! There hasn't been any change at all! This kid is as bad as ever!

Why do you think he went forward if he really didn't mean it?
Pete Moss

Dear Brother Moss,

Hold everything! How do you know that Scott's conversion wasn't real? We're told in Scripture that only God can see a person's heart.

When a child gets saved, he's a new baby in Christ, same as anyone else. He simply needs to grow in his new Christian life. Sometimes the change is very evident, sometimes not.

What Scott needs is an adult who cares enough to see that he gets the follow-up that he needs. He needs someone to pray for him, teach him and encourage him.

Don't give up on Scott until he's had the opportunity to grow! Some kids just go through the motions of receiving Christ, but most are very sincere.

For the kids,

Andy

Dear Andy,

Is it really worth it? I teach in Children's Church, and I'm just not sure that it's worth the trouble.

I spend hours every week cutting out flannelgraph, making handouts, and baking cookies when I could very well be doing something more productive. I'd quit this week, but I know they'd have a hard time getting someone to take my place.

Should I quit? I've been in Children's Church long enough.
Shirley Knott

Dear Miss Knott,

I think you know the answer before I even tell you. So I won't.

But do let me say this—every hour invested in Children's Church will one day be rewarded in a fantastic way. The Lord does keep records, you know.

But think about this: if you spent every Sunday for the next fifty years in Children's Church and only one child got saved, it would be worth it a thousand times over! When a child gets saved, it's for eternity!

It's normal to become discouraged from time to time. It's a problem every teacher faces. When you are tempted to hand the lesson manual (and flannelgraph figures) to a replacement, remember that your job is the most important in the world.

Andy

6.

COUNSELING WITH CHILDREN AT THE INVITATION

In Chapter 4 we considered the most effective ways to present the Bible lesson. We learned that the lesson must be carefully planned and must be built around a specific teaching aim. This aim gives unity and direction to our teaching, enabling us to meet the students' needs. We found that the lesson must be on the pupils' level, utilizing language they will understand and illustrations to which they will relate. We also

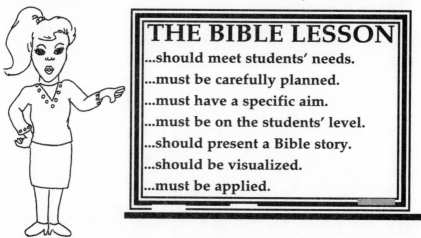

THE BIBLE LESSON
...should meet students' needs.
...must be carefully planned.
...must have a specific aim.
...must be on the students' level.
...should present a Bible story.
...should be visualized.
...must be applied.

found that the lesson is most effective when built around a Bible story, that it should always be visualized, and that it must be applied to the lives of the students.

Then in Chapter 5 we took a look at presenting the Gospel and how to teach God's plan of salvation most effectively to boys and girls. The gospel message must be kept simple, and we must use understandable terminology. Our presentation is most effective when we use visual aids, and we must always use the Scriptures. We know that review is always vital, and this applies especially to presenting the Gospel to children.

The Gospel Presentation

1. Present the message in each Junior Church service.
2. Keep it simple and use understandable terminology.
3. Visualize your presentation of the Gospel.
4. Always use Scripture!
5. Review, review, review!
6. Pray for the work of the Holy Spirit in the hearts of your students.

Now that we've considered the Bible lesson and the presentation of the plan of salvation, let's consider how to lead the students to act upon the truth that has been presented.

The Bible lesson has come to a conclusion. We've used the Word of God to teach and challenge the hearts of our Primaries and Juniors, and now it's time to encourage the students to be doers of the Word, to put the truths they've learned into practice.

If we've taught a salvation lesson, we want to direct the unsaved child to respond and ask Christ to be his Saviour. If the message has been directed to the saved child, we want to lead him to action, to encourage him to make a decision, to integrate the Bible truth into his life. This part of the Children's Church service is often referred to as the *invitation.*

The invitation in Children's Church is a brief period of time at the close of the Bible lesson when you ask the students to respond to your teaching with some specific action. Was the lesson on witnessing? Then the invitation will give the students an opportunity to respond by making a commitment to share the Gospel with others. Was it a salvation message? Then you'll give a salvation invitation, inviting interested students to receive Christ as Saviour that very day.

The invitation is vital, yet this is the very point at which many teachers fail. If God has used our teaching to impact the student's heart and life, then we must show the student how to obey the voice of the Lord, how to follow through on what he has learned. The invitation enables the child to translate truth into action.

Here's how the invitation is usually conducted. At the close of the lesson, the teacher will ask the students to bow their heads while they consider the truths of the lesson. He might direct them to make a promise to God silently, or he might ask for some outward response to show that they are making that decision. If the desired decision is for salvation or other response requiring personal counseling, he will invite them to leave their seats and meet a teacher for further counseling.

Here's how to conduct such an invitation:

Plan your invitation at least ten or fifteen minutes before dismissal. This will give your workers time to counsel with any children who might respond. The counselors will not need to fear interruption and will not be hurried.

Plan other teaching activities to follow the invitation so that the Children's Church service continues after the counselors and students have left the room. This is the ideal time for the Bible review game.

The invitation must be voluntary. As you attempt to lead your students into making a decision for Christ, remember that the decision must be their own. If the Holy Spirit is not leading the child to action, why should we attempt to force the issue? Never *pressure* a child into making a decision.

A number of years ago my wife and I worked in a large Junior Church with several hundred students. Each week at the close of the Bible lesson the director gave a high-pressure invitation. The students who raised their hands for salvation were then brought forward by the workers, whether they wanted to come or not! This type of invitation is not only inappropriate, but it is unethical and wrong. The invitation for children must be voluntary. Allow the Holy Spirit to work in each child's heart and draw him to the Saviour.

The invitation must be clear. Be very clear and specific when you give an invitation for children. Make the objective of the invitation very obvious. Are you inviting unsaved children to come forward and talk with someone regarding receiving Christ as Saviour? Are you asking the saved child to commit himself to being a witness for the Lord? Are you asking him to promise God that he will be obedient to his parents? Make certain that the students understand what decision you are asking them to make.

Why give an invitation for the child to ask God to make him or her a better Christian? Why not invite the child to commit himself or herself to set aside ten minutes each day to read the Bible and pray?

Be specific. Why give an invitation for the child to ask God to give him compassion for the lost? Instead, why not give an invitation for the child to commit himself to witness to one friend during the coming week or to give out one or two gospel tracts? Make the invitation clear and specific. The students must understand what you are asking them to do.

Then be very specific as to how the child is to respond. If he is willing to commit himself to being a witness, how do you want him to respond? Should he raise his hand to let you know, bow his head and pray right in his seat, or come forward to pray with a worker? If God is speaking to the heart of the unsaved student, how is he to let you know so that he may be counseled?

Be very specific in your instructions at the invitation so that the children who wish to respond know exactly what to do.

The invitation should be brief. There's no need to sing eighteen stanzas of "Just as I Am" during a Children's Church invitation. If God is speaking to the heart of a child, he or she will usually respond quickly. Children don't have all the pride and other hang-ups of adults to keep them from responding. Don't belabor the Children's Church invitation. If God is speaking, the kids will respond. If not, don't attempt to push for a decision.

It's very appropriate to use music for the invitation. Perhaps you will want the class to sing two or three verses of "I Have Decided to Follow Jesus" as you conduct the invitation, but do keep it brief.

Again, let me emphasize that the Children's Church invitation must be completely voluntary, that it should be brief, and that you must make your instructions very clear and specific. Plan the invitation at least ten or fifteen minutes before the end of your program, and plan a Bible game or other learning activity to take place following the invitation. Depend on the Lord as you present the Children's Church invitation. Allow Him to work through you to bring your students to Himself.

And now let's consider what happens following the invitation. Suppose two children have come forward at the invitation expressing a desire to receive Jesus as their Saviour. What happens next?

> **The Junior Church Invitation:**
> 1. **Voluntary**
> 2. **Specific**
> 3. **Brief**

As the Children's Church program continues, the two students who have responded are led to counseling rooms by two trained counselors. These workers will use their Bibles to answer any questions the children may have regarding salvation and then will lead them to receive Christ as their Saviour if they are ready and understand.

The counseling room will probably be a Sunday school classroom, but it should be a quiet room that is a bit isolated from the Children's Church room so that those who are counseled are not distracted by the Bible review game and other activities taking place in Children's Church. If at least two groups of children and workers are present, it is best to close the classroom door to shut out distractions. If, however, the counselor will be alone with the child, it is best to leave the door ajar just a few inches so that there is never any suspicion of wrongdoing.

The counselor should be seated facing the classroom door with the child directly across from him. This places the child's back to the door so that any distractions from the outside are kept to a minimum. If several teachers are counseling children in one classroom, each teacher sits

with his back to a corner of the room, with the students facing the corner. Again, this places any activity in the room behind the child and minimizes the distractions as the child is counseled.

The counselor should be warm and friendly. Ask the child's name and then use it frequently. Make small talk for a moment or two, inquiring about the child's school, family, hobbies, etc. This relaxes the student, gets him talking and responding, and helps him get to know you.

Present the entire plan of salvation again using your Bible. Turn the Bible toward the child so that he may read the verses as you quote them or read them upside down. Do not be in a hurry as you carefully explain the gospel message to the student. Even though the child may have heard it moments before in the Children's Church lesson, take the time to present it again thoroughly and prayerfully.

Watch the child's eyes as you present the plan of salvation. When question marks appear, stop and explain or review the concept that the child does not understand. If you have taken a moment or two to get the child talking and responding before you get into the Scriptures, hopefully he will feel free to ask you questions as you proceed.

Ask the child questions as you explain God's plan of salvation. It's usually best to stay away from "yes" or "no" questions and make use of questions that begin with the word *why*. "Why do you need to be saved?" "Why did Jesus die for you?"

As you ask questions of the child, you are helping him think through this important decision he is about to make. The questions help focus his attention on the matter at hand, and his answers help you evaluate his comprehension of the gospel plan.

Once you have presented the entire plan of salvation, lead the child to receive Jesus as his Saviour. Have him simply bow his head and pray, asking Jesus to save him from his sins. If he does not know how to pray, you

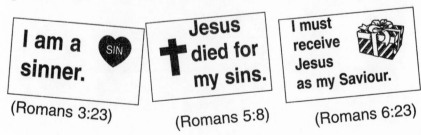

I am a sinner. (SIN)
(Romans 3:23)

Jesus died for my sins.
(Romans 5:8)

I must receive Jesus as my Saviour.
(Romans 6:23)

might even need to help him with the words to say, making certain that he is willing and understands that he is the one who must receive Jesus by faith.

If, however, the child is not ready or does not understand, *do not push for a decision.* Ask God for guidance and discernment as you lead children to Christ. Carefully evaluate the child's answers as you ask questions during the presentation of the Gospel. If the child is not ready, do not try to push him into a decision that will be meaningless and will later cause confusion.

Simply close by saying, "Tina, I'm glad you came and talked with me today, but I don't think you understand everything we talked about. Come back again next week, and if you want to talk with me again, I'll be glad to talk with you. Receiving Jesus as your Saviour is the most important decision you will ever make. I'm going to be praying that you'll understand and be saved soon."

With a closing such as this, you are making it obvious that Tina did not get saved just because she came forward and talked with you, and you are also leaving the door open for her to respond when she is ready.

Before you send the child back to Children's Church, pray aloud for her. Again, as you pray, make it clear to Tina that she did not get saved simply by coming forward or talking with you. Once you have finished dealing with the child, allow her to return to her seat in Children's Church.

When dealing with the child who does understand and is ready to receive Christ as Saviour, lead him to pray and ask Jesus to save him, and then take a few moments to deal with assurance. Briefly review the gospel plan and the decision the child has just made, then go back to Scripture for verses of assurance. John 5:24, John 10:28, Romans 10:13 and I John 5:11–13 are good Scriptures to use. Do not tell the child that he is now saved; show him the Scriptures and allow the Holy Spirit to give him this assurance.

It's also good to leave the child with some follow-up material—tracts or booklets that will give him more information and encouragement regarding his new Christian life. Your local Christian bookstore will have these available. As with any material that you give to children, read through these to make sure that they are scriptural and accurate.

Leading a child to Christ is the greatest joy you will ever experience as a teacher and the most crucial part of your entire ministry, so do it carefully and prayerfully. Ask God to use you to bring children to Himself!

As I enter that beautiful city
And the children around me appear,
I want to hear some of them tell me,
"It was you that invited me here."

COUNSELING AT THE INVITATION:
1. Use a quiet room.
2. Be friendly; use the child's name.
3. Present the plan of salvation.
4. Ask questions.
5. Allow the child to ask questions.
6. Do not push for a decision.
7. Lead the child to pray, if ready.
8. Use follow-up material.

and next pages

Evaluating the Invitation

YES   NO

___   ___   1. Do I plan the invitation early enough in the service to allow my counselors adequate time to deal with the children who respond?

___   ___   2. Do I always remember that the children's response to the invitation must be voluntary?

___   ___   3. Do I allow the Holy Spirit to work, rather than pressing for decisions?

___   ___   4. Are my invitations clear?

___   ___   5. Do the students understand the decision I am asking them to make?

___   ___   6. Do they know what to do if they want to respond?

___   ___   7. Am I careful with the terminology I use?

___   ___   8. Are my invitations for children brief?

Counselor's Checklist

YES   NO

___ ___ 1. Was I warm and friendly as I talked with the child?

___ ___ 2. Did I remember to ask the child's name and use it?

___ ___ 3. Did I remember to make "small talk" with the child for a moment or two to get to know him?

___ ___ 4. Did the child feel free to ask questions?

___ ___ 5. Was the counseling room quiet and free from distractions?

___ ___ 6. Did I use my Bible as I presented the plan of salvation, allowing the child to read along with me?

___ ___ 7. Did I ask thought-provoking questions as I proceeded?

___ ___ 8. Did I seek God's guidance?

___ ___ 9. Was I careful not to push for a decision?

___ ___ 10. If the child was not ready or did not understand, did I encourage him to respond again later?

___ ___ 11. Did I get follow-up information on the child who did pray to receive Christ?

___ ___ 12. Did I give him follow-up literature?

___ ___ 13. Did I leave him with an assurance verse?

Ask Andy!

Dear Andy,

Our church runs two buses and a van. We have a fairly good Sunday school and an adequate Children's Church program in which my wife and I both serve.

The problem is this: a couple of other churches in town run buses, and they are always stealing our kids. We'll have a family of kids faithfully ride our bus for awhile, then one of the other churches will visit them, and poof! They're gone—off to the other church! Before long, they're not attending either church.

When the people from the other churches canvas for new riders, it doesn't matter if the kids are already faithful to our church. They put the pressure on our kids to "just come visit" one Sunday, offering prizes for riding the bus. Isn't there anything we can do?

I guess it wouldn't bother me so much if our kids became faithful at another church. But they don't. Once they start visiting around, it seems that it's not long before they become "drop-outs."

Phil O'Dendron

Dear Phil,

When a minister proselytes another minister's members, it's referred to as "sheep-stealing." Sounds like that is what's going on here.

There is not a whole lot you can do about it, except this—work overtime to build the very best kids' program in town! Your Sunday school and Children's Church shouldn't be "fairly good" or "adequate": they should both be "world-class"! Work on developing a Children's Church that is so outstanding your kids wouldn't dream of going anywhere else! And plan lots of outings and activities with the kids; this helps build relationships and establishes a real loyalty to your ministry.

Then do your best to make sure that none of your own workers are guilty of "sheep-stealing."

Andy

Dear Andy,

We have an unusual problem—the adult choir uses our Children's Church room for practice just before the morning service (we have the only piano other than the one in the church sanctuary). As a result of the choir practice, we start Children's Church about five minutes late every Sunday.

And the kids don't just sit quietly while the choir is using our room, either.

Anyway, by the time the choir leaves our room, the kids are pretty wound up, and we get off to a rough start every Sunday morning.

We've tried to talk with the choir director about it, but he just shrugs it off. I don't think he sees the kids' ministry as being very important. Any suggestions?

Dinah Sorrh

Dear Dinah,

Three simple solutions immediately came to mind: (1) march your Children's Church kids over to the sanctuary and let them use the choir loft to practice Children's Church songs while you are waiting for the choir to get through; (2) temporarily retune the Children's Church piano so horribly that no one in the choir could ever stay on key; (3) have your Children's Church kids out-sing the choir every time they practice!

Seriously, you do have a major problem, and I understand your frustration. In many churches, the children's ministries are not regarded as being as important as the adult ministries. Hence, problems arise such as you have just described.

Schedule an appointment with your pastor, possibly including your deacon board or Christian education committee, and explain the problem. If you get no action, you might even take it just a step further.

Have a friend videotape the next choir rehearsal, zeroing in on the discipline problems that are being created. Then make a second appointment and show your tape. No Children's Church leaders should ever have to go through what you are enduring, but do try to keep a cheerful attitude while you search for a solution.

Andy

7.
BIBLE REVIEW GAMES

Over twenty years ago a student in a little church in southern California introduced me to one of the most fantastic teaching tools I had ever seen. This one method has done more for my Children's Church ministry than just about any other. I'm still excited about Bible review games.

Bible games can bring excitement and life to any Children's Church ministry, causing the students to enjoy class time like never before. Bible learning accelerates in such a teaching environment, and attendance soars. Once you get hooked on Bible games, you'll never want to go back to the dreary drudgery of teaching without them!

Briefly, here's what Bible games are all about. The teacher prepares a dozen key review questions from the day's lesson. After the lesson, or after the invitation following the lesson, the class is divided into two teams, and the teacher gives the questions orally. The student giving a correct answer comes to the flannel board to attempt to score points for his or her team. You and the students will both enjoy the game time! As one teacher from Michigan wrote, "Teachers who have not seen the Bible games may not realize how much fun and how exciting they really are!"

I firmly believe that every teacher of children should make maximum use of Bible games. Here's why:

Bible games sparkle with fun and excitement! If the kids in your Children's Church were to evaluate your teaching ministry, how would your program rate? On an enjoyment scale of 1 to 10 (with spinach casserole rating a 1 and a trip to Six Flags rating a 10), would your Children's Church score above a 2 or a 3? Would

Joey sez:

"I like Bible games! They're really cool! I always listen carefully to the Bible lesson so I can answer the questions."

you even dare to hope for a 7 or an 8?

Why shouldn't Children's Church rate a 9 or a 10? I firmly believe that teaching children should be fun, both for the student and the teacher. If you're afraid of the word *fun,* then use the word *enjoyable.* Why should Children's Church ever have a reputation for being boring?

Start using Bible games, and you and the kids will begin to enjoy your ministry like never before. The educational experts tell us that is the ideal learning environment—a class that the pupil enjoys. Bible games make learning fun and exciting for both students and teacher!

Bible games are an excellent way to review. The educators tell us that one-third of our teaching time should be spent in review. Repetition is one of the keys to learning. And yet, most Children's Church leaders spend little or no time at all in review! We constantly teach and preach, moving from one Bible concept to the next without pausing to find out if our students are retaining what we have taught.

If you stand up after the Bible message in Children's Church and announce, "It's time to review the message," you'll be met with groans of dismay. Instead, simply announce, "We're going to play a Bible game! It's called 'Zonk'! Boys against the girls!" Your class will respond with

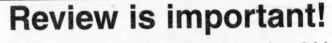

Review is important!
One-third of our teaching time should be spent in review.

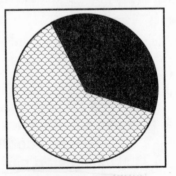

New Material

Review

Teaching Time

enthusiasm! Review is important, and Bible games are the most effective way I know to do it.

Bible games encourage class participation. An unresponsive class is one of the biggest frustrations a teacher can ever face. It's tough to try to teach when the students give the impression they would much rather be somewhere else. Kids who refuse to sing, never respond to your questions, and pay no attention during the lesson can make even the most dedicated teacher think about resigning. Teaching can be a real joy, but not when you have an unresponsive class.

Why settle for such a dismal teaching situation? Use Bible games and draw those kids out of their shells! Even the most uncooperative students will be intrigued by the games and begin participating in spite of themselves. And then, they get involved in the other aspects of class time as well.

Bible games involve the entire class. A review game can be used with any size Children's Church. A group of four kids can play; even a group of four hundred can play! The entire class gets involved. Each time you ask a question, each student frames the answer in his or her own mind, hoping to be the one chosen to answer the question.

Bible games help the teacher evaluate his teaching. It's easy to fall into the trap of thinking that you taught effectively just because the students were relatively quiet during the lesson, but just how much are your students learning? You may think they're listening, but are they? Would you like to find out?

The Bible game elicits verbal feedback from the students which is essential for an accurate evaluation of our effectiveness as teachers. Carefully worded questions cause the student to review the lesson in his own words, allowing the teacher even keener insights into her students' progress.

Bible games can be used to correct wrong impressions. When a student (or perhaps the entire class) has misunderstood some concept from the Bible message, that fact will come out during the Bible game. The teacher then has the opportunity at that point to restate or reword the idea, correcting the wrong impressions or misunderstandings that exist in the minds of the pupils.

7 Reasons to Use Bible Games

1. Bible Games are fun and exciting!
2. Bible Games are a fantastic way to review.
3. Bible Games encourage class participation.
4. Bible Games involve the entire class.
5. Bible Games help evaluate our teaching.
6. Bible Games can correct wrong impressions.
7. Bible Games reinforce the lesson.

Bible games reinforce the lesson. The games are always most effective when the teacher writes the questions in advance, using carefully worded key questions to reinforce and reemphasize the important points of the lesson. Use the questions to stress the key facts from the Bible story and the main points of application. Key questions that have some thought behind them cause your students to think and cause an effective lesson to have even greater impact on the students' lives.

Effective use of Bible games

A Bible game is an effective tool that you and your students will thoroughly enjoy—if you use it properly. The Bible game is most effective when used to review lesson material that has previously been taught, rather than choosing questions at random from the Bible or a quiz book.

At the close of the lesson or invitation following the message, introduce the game for the day and explain the rules. Divide the class into two teams: boys against girls, odd grades against even, or whatever method is efficient and fair.

Choose one of your pupils as the starter for the game. As each question is given, the starter will ring a bell, honk a bicycle horn, or give some other signal for the pupils to respond to your question. The pupils raise their hands or stand (whichever way you instruct them), and a designated adult worker selects the pupil to answer the question. If the pupil answers the question correctly, he or she comes to the flannel board to play the game and attempt to score points for the team.

When a student cannot answer the question or answers incorrectly, repeat the question and allow another student (from either team) to answer it.

It's best for an adult to keep score. At the conclusion of the game, announce the team scores and lead the winning team in a quick cheer.

Here are a few simple rules to follow for the most effective use of Bible games:

Make the game time fun and enjoyable. Join in the fun with your kids! Get excited when they score and empathize with them when they don't. When your students see you as a person who can lead them in a time of fun, effective teacher/student bonds begin to form. Bible games are fun, and Children's Church can be an enjoyable time for both teachers and students!

Write your questions in advance of Children's Church. Word them carefully. Always remember your objectives as you use the Bible games: to review and reinforce the Bible lesson, to evaluate the effectiveness of the lesson, and to have an opportunity to correct any wrong impressions or misunderstandings the students may have. There's no need here for "trick questions." Plan your questions carefully; good questions require thought and preparation but pay off in the form of effective teaching.

Use the Bible game to review your lesson. When I first started using Bible games in Children's Church, I chose questions at random from all parts of the Bible, but then I began to see how effective the game could be as a lesson review. Now I always draw my questions directly from the Bible message for that day.

Use Bible fact and Bible application questions. Some of your review questions will deal with the basic facts of the Bible story, while others should address the personal application of the lesson. The second type of question encourages the student to use the Bible knowledge he is acquiring and apply it to life's decisions and situations.

Again, good questions are vital. They are the backbone of the entire Bible game. It is impossible to have an effective Bible game with poorly-worded questions.

Accept correct answers only. It is imperative that you accept only correct answers. If a child fails to answer or gives an incorrect answer, do not allow the other students to ridicule that child.

Repeat each correct answer so that all can hear. The purpose of the Bible game is to educate. Before the student comes to the board to play the game, repeat his correct answer so that every student hears it.

On occasion you will ask a question that no student can answer, even after several tries. When this happens, always give the correct answer before you drop the question and move on to the next.

Make sure that every child has a chance to participate—involve the entire class. Many times I've had a game spotter who wanted to select students from only the front row or one particular side. Be alert, and make sure that any student can participate, no matter where he or she is seated. Select from both teams.

The class "brain" may seem to expect to be allowed to answer every question. Allow him to answer one, but be sure to include the others as well.

Set a time limit. Bible games are a lot of fun. They're exciting, and it's thrilling to see your students get involved. But be sure to wrap up the game while interest is at a peak and the students are wanting more. I've known teachers who play a Bible game for the last half hour of Children's Church!

A dozen questions are usually about right for the length of game you want. Ten or twelve review questions, plus the time spent at the game board, will usually involve about ten or twelve minutes of class time.

Use a variety of games. As you know by now, one of my favorite words is *VARIETY*. VARIETY is what keeps our teaching fresh and exciting, and keeps the students enthusiastic about our Children's Church program.

This chapter contains ideas for nine Bible games. Don't get locked into just one or two of the games; make and play them all. Play one particular game for two or three weeks, then file it away carefully and use another, and then another. In a few months, get out the first games and use them again. Your Children's Church will have VARIETY, and your students will appreciate you for it!

Effective Use of Bible Games

1. **Make the games fun!**
2. **Write your questions carefully.**
3. **Use the game to review your lesson.**
4. **Use both Bible fact and application questions.**
5. **Accept correct answers only.**
6. **Repeat each correct answer.**
7. **Involve the entire class.**
8. **Set a time limit.** ~ a dozen questions/minutes
9. **Use a VARIETY of games.**

Ready for that first game? Let's start with one of my all-time favorites!

Game #1—YOUR GUESS?

Your Guess? gives each student answering a Bible question three separate chances to score points for his or her team. The child chooses one of thirty-two stars from the game board, then guesses the number on the back of that star—100, 200 or 300. The teacher then turns the star over, revealing the number on the back. If the student's guess is

correct, she receives the points for her team. If the guess is incorrect, no points are given. If the star is turned over to reveal the word "Bonus," the child automatically receives the number of points she guessed—100, 200 or 300. Each child chooses three stars on a turn, with the possibility of scoring on all three stars.

Making the game. Cut thirty-two 3" stars from several bright colors of posterboard. (Do not use construction paper as it quickly fades.) Stencil the numeral 100 on the backs of eight stars, 200 on eight stars, and 300 on eight stars. Stencil the word "BONUS" on the backs of the remaining stars. (If you have a computer with a simple graphics program, it is very easy to make some very attractive star cards with the numerals on them.)

In place of the stars, you may want to use apples, strawberries, butterflies, smiley faces, etc. Teaching supply stores carry a number of ready-made bulletin board aids that are perfect for this game.

Laminate the stars (apples, etc.) and fasten small pieces of felt or Velcro above and below the numerals so that the card will adhere to your flannel board. Make the **Your Guess?** title card (complete with lamination and felt), and your game is ready.

Playing the game. Place the title card in the center of your flannel board and scatter the thirty-two stars at random across the board. Choose a game starter from your students, a game spotter from your adult workers, and explain the rules to your class.

At the conclusion of the game, plan a bonus question for each team. Have each student choose four stars, and double the points for each correct guess!

Game #2—UP or DOWN?

Here's another simple game that will get an enthusiastic response from your students! The boy or girl who answers the Bible question correctly comes to the flannel board and chooses a group of three colored squares. The teacher flips the center square, revealing a number between 10 and 100. The student then chooses one of the two remaining squares from that group, either above or below his number

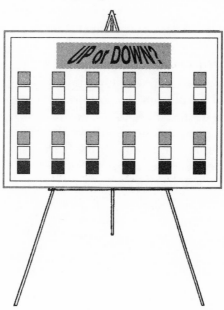

square. The teacher flips the card the student has chosen, revealing a *B* or a *G* and assigning the points from that turn to the boys' or girls' team. No matter which team is at the board, either team can receive the points! If the up or down card reveals a star, the points automatically go to the team of the student at the board.

Making the game. Cut thirty-six 3" squares from posterboard, twelve each of yellow, red and blue. On the backs of ten of the yellow cards, stencil numerals between 10 and 100, and stencil question marks on two remaining yellow cards. Stencil five *B*'s, five *G*'s and two stars on the twelve red cards, and five *B*'s, five *G*'s, and two stars on the blue cards. Laminate the cards, then attach flocking or felt so they will adhere to the flannel board. Make the **UP or DOWN?** title card for the game, and you're ready to play **UP or DOWN?**

(The squares may be made from felt rather than posterboard, using

vinyl numerals and letters. This removes the necessity for laminating the cards, and the felt adheres well to the flannel board.)

Playing the game. Position all thirty-six squares on the flannel board in groups of three as in the illustration, placing the red squares on top in each group, the blue on the bottom. After a student answers the Bible question, he or she comes to the board and chooses one group of three squares. You remove the center (yellow) square for the student, announcing the number of points on the back. (If you find a question mark [?], the student chooses a score from 10 to 100, not knowing, of course, which team will receive the points.)

The student then chooses "up" or "down," and you remove the appropriate card, announcing which team receives the points. As the child at the board is deciding up or down, the other students will usually begin calling "Up! Up!" or "Down! Down!" There is no need to discourage this—(it actually helps build the excitement) unless the class begins to get out of control.

At the conclusion of the game, plan a bonus question for each team. Double the points on these final two turns. (If a child finds a question mark on a bonus question, allow him to select up to 200 points.)

Game #3—RED LIGHT, GREEN LIGHT

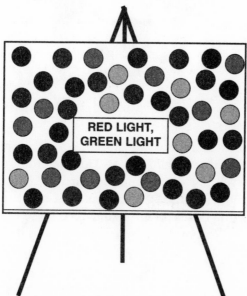

This Bible game has never failed to be a hit with kids and teachers alike! It's easy to make, simple to use, and about as much fun and excitement as one class can handle!

The student answering the game question correctly comes to the flannel board and selects one of forty-eight bright felt circles. The teacher removes the circle, revealing a number on the back. A "Green Light" doubles the points on the next two choices. The student may continue choosing circles and scoring points as long as he likes! But if he chooses a "Red Light," his turn ends, and he loses all his points. When a student is at the game board, the excitement in class is electrifying!

Making the game. Purchase 9" x 12" felt squares in six bright colors from your local fabric store. (Be sure to buy good-quality felt; some of the cheaper stuff is almost thin enough to read through.) Cut eight 3" circles from each color for a total of forty-eight circles.

At your local office supply or school supply retailer, buy sheets of

one-inch, white vinyl stick-on numerals.   You will need a total of thirty-six numerals.

Set aside two circles from each color for a total of twelve circles. On the back of nine of these, color a large, solid red dot, or "Red Light." Draw a large "Green Light" on the other three circles. In the center of each of the remaining thirty-six circles, place a numeral from 1 to 10. Make a **"Red Light, Green Light"** name card and put felt or flocking on the back. Your **Red Light, Green Light** game is ready for action!

To store the game, cut the tab off a letter-size file folder, then slip it inside a 9" x 12" manilla envelope. Label the envelope with the name of the game.

Playing the game. Before time for the Bible game, scatter the forty-eight circles at random across your flannel board with the numbers, "Red Lights" and "Green Lights" hidden on the back. As the student selects circles, announce each number, then announce her total points for that turn, giving her the option of stopping or continuing. Once she decides to stop, announce her score to the adult scorekeeper, who records the points. When the points go to the scoreboard, they are permanent. A "Red Light" later in the game does not erase these points.

At the conclusion of the game, plan a bonus question for each team. Double the points on these two final questions! Announce the bonus before asking the question.

Perhaps you have a large Children's Church. Play **Red Light, Green Light** the way I do, on a giant 4' x 8' flannel board. The circles are seven inches in diameter, with two-inch numerals on the back. I use the game with crowds of six hundred kids and more!

Game #4--DOMINO DUNKING

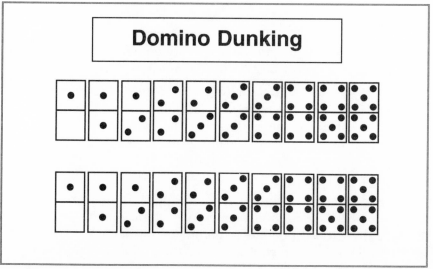

This is a new Bible game that we have been using for just a short while, but the kids have responded with quite a bit of enthusiasm when we play it. I think it's going to become a favorite! The dominos in the top row are the girls'; the bottom row is for the boys. The first team to "knock down" all ten of the other team's dominos wins.

The student answering the review question comes forward and chooses two game cards, which assign to him two numbers from 1 to 6. He may then "knock down" two of the other team's dominos that correspond with those numbers, or combine the numbers to remove one domino with a higher number. A choose card allows him to remove any one domino he selects.

Making the game. Make ten 3" x 6" dominos from blue felt, numbering them from 1 to 10 with black marker or liquid embroidery. Make ten similar dominos from red or pink felt, or simply make them from colored 3 x 5 cards (cut to 2 1/2" wide). Laminate them if you wish, and fasten felt or flocking to the back of each. (The dominos go on the board with the numbers showing, so be sure

| 1 | 2 | 3 | 4 | 5 | 6 |

to put the felt on the opposite side.)

Make twenty-four game cards: four each of the numerals 1-5, two of numbers 6, and two marked "Choose." **Domino Dunking** is ready to play!

Playing the game. Position all twenty dominos in two horizontal rows across your flannel board with the numbers showing. Spread the twenty-four game cards facedown on a nearby table or lectern, select the game starter and spotter, and explain the rules to the kids.

In this game it is imperative that the questions alternate evenly between the two teams. If a child gives an incorrect answer, select another student from the same team to answer.

As each student selects his two cards, give him the option of removing two dominos or combining the numbers to "knock down" the higher numbered domino that corresponds to the sum of the two cards. Remove the selected domino or dominos from the game board. If a child draws a game card with a number that has already been removed, he does not draw another card.

At the conclusion of the game, plan a bonus question for each team. The students then draw three cards. These may be used in any combination to remove 1, 2 or 3 dominos.

In the event of a tie, select two students to come forward and each draw one game card. The highest number wins, with a "Choose" card taking precedence over any number card.

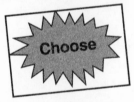

Game #5—WORD SCRAMBLE

This game does not require the use of a flannel board. Each student answering a question comes forward and selects seven letter cards. She then has thirty-five seconds to make a proper English word using as many of the letters as possible, with certain letters scoring more points than others. When she completes a word within the allotted time, she then chooses a game card, which may increase her score.

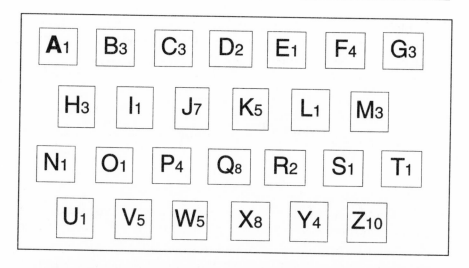

Making the game. Cut ninety-six 2" squares of white posterboard. (This requires just one 22" x 28" sheet.) Stencil a 1" letter on each card, with a 1/2" point value beside it, following the chart above. Make the following number of cards of each letter:

A - 9, B - 3, C - 2, D - 4, E - 10, F - 2, G - 3, H - 2, I - 7, J - 1, K - 1, L - 5, M - 2, N - 4, O - 8, P - 2, Q - 1, R - 5, S - 5, T - 6, U - 4, V - 2, W - 2, X - 1, Y - 2, Z - 1, and blank - 2.

The white posterboard is fairly durable, and should not need to be laminated.

Now make twelve 3" x 5" game cards from colored posterboard. Make two each of the double- and triple-word cards, and two each of the double- and triple-letter cards. Mark a numeral at the bottom of the double- and triple-letter cards to indicate which letter value in the word is to be doubled or tripled. And last, make four "Sorry" cards.

Playing the game. Spread all ninety-six letter cards facedown on a table or desk, fanning the twelve game cards facedown nearby. Select a game starter and spotter, and make certain that someone has a stopwatch or other timing device that can mark thirty-five to forty seconds. (I use a large, highly-visible, floating hourglass that runs for thirty-five seconds.) Explain the rules for the game, then give the first question.

As the child selects his seven letter cards, place them in the chalk tray

Double Letter Score (2)	Double Word Score	Triple Letter Score (1)	Triple Word Score	SORRY	SORRY
Double Letter Score (4)	Double Word Score	Triple Letter Score (3)	Triple Word Score	SORRY!	SORRY!

of the classroom chalkboard, lean them up against your visual board, or place them in some place where the entire class can view them. When the last letter is chosen and displayed, start the timer.

It is permissible for the team to help the student choose a word. A blank may be used as any letter to make a word, but scores no points. When the word is completed, add the point values on each letter card that was used and announce the total.

At that point, have the student select a game card, and announce his final score. A double- or triple-letter card multiplies the points on only the card indicated; for example, a *(4)* on a double-letter card indicates that the fourth letter in the word is to have double value. A "Sorry" card does not affect the child's score.

At the conclusion of the game, double the points on the final question for each team.

Game #6—TIC-TAC-TOE LIVE

Here's a game that's older than your grandmother, but with a fun, new twist. When playing **Tic-Tac-Toe Live,** the students become the X's and O's! Players do not choose which square they want on the game grid; their position is assigned by a game card.

It's different, to say the least! This is one of the easiest games to prepare—the only equipment needed is nine chairs and nine game cards.

Making the game. Duplicate the game cards below on colored card stock, or simply write them out on nine 3 x 5 index cards. Obtain nine chairs for the game grid, and you're ready to play **Tic-Tac-Toe Live!**

Back Row	Center Row	Front Row
Left Column	Center Column	Right Column
Your Choice	Your Choice	Your Choice

Playing the game. Arrange the nine chairs in three rows of three, and spread the nine game cards facedown on a nearby table or lectern. Choose your game starter and spotter, and introduce the game to your students.

As each child answers a question, he or she comes forward and chooses a game card, then turns it over and takes the seat indicated by the card. A "back row" card would allow the child to take any empty seat in the last three chairs, "right column" would designate any empty seat on the right-hand ends of the rows, etc. "Your choice" allows the student to select any empty seat.

The questions must alternate between the two teams. As in regular **Tic-Tac-Toe,** the first team to get three in a row wins. In the event of a "cat's game" (tie), place the game cards facedown again and continue to play. All nine seats will be filled at this point, so the student drawing the card may select any seat on the row or column indicated. The occupant of that seat must relinquish his place to the newcomer.

The only drawback to **Tic-Tac-Toe Live** is that it is possible for one team to win as early as the fifth question. In the event of an extremely quick game, clear the chairs, replace the game cards, and play a second round.

Game #7—GO FOR THE GOLD!

This Bible game is simple but fun, especially during the year of the Olympics. Students answer questions, then draw a medal from a grab bag, receiving gold, silver or bronze. The various medals have different point values, and the team with the highest score wins.

Making the game. Obtain fifteen large disks of identical size (large checkers, canning jar lids, etc.). Spray paint five of the disks gold, five silver and five bronze. (The spray paint may be purchased inexpensively at any discount department store.) Place the "medals" in a grab bag, and the game is ready.

Playing the game. Let the two teams represent two nations. As each "athlete" answers a question, he or she comes forward and chooses one "medal" from the grab bag. At the game's conclusion, plan one double question for each team, with each child choosing two medals.

Scores are totaled with each gold medal worth 300 points; silver, 200; and bronze, 100.

Game #8—FISHING

This game is not original with me, but it's a lot of fun for the students, and I must include it here. I've seen many different teachers use the **Fishing** game, but I suppose it would be impossible to trace the idea to its originator.

The teacher hands a small fishing rod (tree limb?) with a horseshoe magnet at the end of a short line to the student answering the Bible question. The student then "fishes" in a paper grocery sack to catch paper fish with paper clip mouths, scoring points for his or her team.

Making the game. Obtain a child's fishing rod (or tree limb) and attach 2' of fishing line, then tie a small horseshoe or round magnet to the end. (The magnets are available at any Radio Shack or toy store.) Make fifteen 5" fish from various colors of posterboard or card stock, stenciling numerals from 10 to 100 on each. (You might even want to make a couple of fish with minus points, which would subtract points from the team's total.)

Playing the game. As the student fishes, allow him to catch only one fish per turn. If the magnet draws up two or more fish at one time, allow the student to keep the fish with the lowest number. (Explain that "it's the big ones that get away.")

As the game progresses, announce each student's score to the scorekeeper. Plan a bonus question for each team at the game's conclusion. Allow the students to catch two or even three fish, or double or triple the points on the final turns.

Variations.

1. You might even play the game with the review questions paperclipped to each fish. Choose students at random to "fish." If the student can answer the question on his fish, his team receives the points.

2. On occasion, slip in two or three fish that say "Choose 1." The student catching one of these fish then selects any one fish from the other team's catch!

3. Prepare two or three fish that say "Double" or "Triple." The student catching one of these bonus fish then casts again and catches another fish, with the points on that fish being doubled or tripled.

121

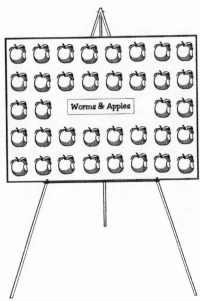

Game #9—WORMS and APPLES

How about one final Bible game for the flannel board? When playing **Worms and Apples**, the student answers a review question, then comes to the board and chooses an apple. The teacher removes the apple, revealing a number (1-10) on the back. The student may continue choosing apples and scoring points for his team as long as he likes, but if he gets a worm, he has to stop and loses all his points! This is a lively game that your Children's Church students will enjoy.

Making the game. Cut thirty-six apples from red posterboard or card stock. Stencil the numerals 1-10 on the back of twenty-seven of the apples and draw a green worm on the back of the remaining nine. Laminate the apples and fasten felt or flannel to the back of each. Make the **Worms and Apples** title card, and the game is ready.

(Another option: Cut the apples from red felt, stenciling the numerals on the back with liquid embroidery. Glue green felt worms to the back of nine apples, or draw the worms with green liquid embroidery.)

Playing the game. Place the title card in the center of your flannel board, then position the apples in five horizontal rows. As each child answers a review question, she comes to the board and begins choosing apples. As you remove each apple for her, announce the point value on the back, announce her total for that turn, then give her the option of stopping or continuing. If she stops before getting a worm, her points go to the scoreboard to stay, unaffected by a worm later in the game. Plan a double question for each team as the game concludes.

Bible games are effective teaching tools!

I trust that the Bible games presented here will be a blessing to your Children's Church ministry as they have been to mine. Once you discover just how much fun and excitement the games can bring to class, how effective they are in reviewing the lesson, and how well the kids will listen because they know that a Bible game will follow the lesson, you'll want to make them a regular part of your Children's Church program.

Teacher, will you use a Bible game in our Junior Church? Please?

Don't wait—get started using this effective teaching tool right away!

As you know by now, I believe that an effective Children's Church program is one that has VARIETY. Don't use puppets every week; plan a puppet show every third or fourth week. Don't show a video, filmstrip or movie every Sunday; once a month is probably often enough. Use Sword drills sparingly; a Sword drill every Sunday is just too often. But check this out—the Bible games are so effective, I use them nearly every Sunday of the year! In a typical year, I suppose I use Bible games fifty Sundays out of fifty-two! They're that effective!

Of course, as in every other part of the program, you want VARIETY in your Bible games. Use one particular game for two or three weeks, then file it away and use another, and then another. After a few months, bring out the first games and use them again. Your class will enjoy the VARIETY.

Many teachers have discovered that these games spark some game ideas of their own.

Two days ago a Children's Church leader in another state called me to share a game idea that he had developed— "OCTOPUS." A lady called us last week and said that she buys the self-stick note pads that come in various shapes: hearts, strawberries, etc. She keeps a pad in her purse. If she needs a Bible game on the spur of the moment, she just whips out a pad and writes numbers, etc., on the back of a number of the pages. Since there is adhesive on the back of each page, she can play the game on a visual board, the wall, or even a door. Talk about creative!

Get started on Bible games today. You'll soon be hooked on this exciting, effective teaching tool, and your Children's Church will never be the same!

Bible Game Checklist

YES NO

___ ___ 1. Do I fully understand the reasons for using Bible review games?

___ ___ 2. Am I using this Bible game as a teaching tool rather than just as a timer-filler?

___ ___ 3. Are my review questions written out?

___ ___ 4. Are they clear?

___ ___ 5. Do they cover the main points of the lesson?

___ ___ 6. Did I avoid "trick questions"?

___ ___ 7. Do I have a combination of Bible fact and Bible application questions?

___ ___ 8. Do I fully understand the rules for this game, so that I can explain it simply to my students?

___ ___ 9. Are all the game pieces in the game folder?

___ ___10. Does my "game spotter" understand the need to choose students from all parts of the classroom and to select evenly from both teams?

___ ___11. Am I prepared to conduct the Bible game with excitement, yet maintain classroom control at all times?

___ ___12. Do I plan to set up the game before class so that my students will not have to wait?

13. When was the last time I used this game in class?

___ ___14. Do I keep a written record?

___ ___15. Do I use a VARIETY of games so that they are always fresh and exciting?

Dear Andy,

The Bible games are great! My Junior Church has come alive, and the kids are asking for more. Now all the Sunday school teachers are borrowing my games.

Where can we find more Bible games?

Foo Ling Yu

Dear Foo Ling,

I'm glad that Junior Church is going so well for you. The games are really something, aren't they?

Standard Publishing has additional books of Bible review games for Sunday school and Junior Church.

Overhead Projector Games contains seven review games on transparencies for the overhead projector, and *More! Overhead Projector Games* has seven more. Both books are excellent resources for any children's ministry.

I wish all questions were as easy as yours.

Andy

Dear Andy,

Are you telling us that Children's Church should be "fun"? Come on! We're preparing our students for adult church, and they sure don't play Bible games over there!

We have a hard enough time getting our kids to listen to the Bible lesson without getting them all stirred up with games and contests.   Personally, I think we need more emphasis on teaching and less emphasis on "fun."

Shirley Taken

Dear Miss Taken,

For the moment, forget that Bible games are fun and that your students will immensely enjoy them.

Instead, focus on the fact that there is a proven teaching method that reviews your lesson effectively, elicits verbal feedback from the students, and reinforces the truths of the lesson. This same method encourages class participation, involves the entire class, and creates the opportunity for the teacher to correct wrong impressions and misunderstandings of scriptural truths.

Would you be willing to try it? I hope so!

If you're still not convinced, slip into a Sunday school class or Children's Church where the teachers use Bible games and just observe for awhile.   One thing you'll notice—THE KIDS WILL BE LISTENING TO THE LESSON! Could you use some help in that area? Need I say more?

For the children,

Andy

Dear Andy,

What would you do if your parents made you go to a Junior Church that was really boring? All they ever do is sing and preach, and a lot of the kids hate it. Some of the kids even hide in the bathroom, but I don't think they're doing right. What should we do?

Willy Makit

Dear Willy,

Thanks for writing. Have your Dad buy a copy of "I Can't Wait Till Sunday Morning!" and give it to your Junior Church teachers. It's available from Sword of the Lord Publishers (1-800-24-SWORD). I hope it helps.

Hang in there, kid.

Your friend,

Andy

Dear Andy,

My wife, Eileen, and I would like to help in Children's Church, but we've been told that we're too old to relate to kids. (I'm sixty-seven, and my wife is, well, a birthday or two behind me. Can you believe it—after forty-five years of marriage, she's still shy about telling her age!)

What do you think? Are we too old? We both love kids, and we'd like to think that there's something we can do.

Ben Dover

Dear Ben,

Who said you're too old? Moses didn't start his ministry until he was eighty! I've noticed in our Children's Church that the kids quickly warm to an older couple and respect them like grandparents.

Single people make excellent Children's Church workers, but I'm always especially glad to have married couples on my staff. Some of our students have never observed a godly marriage with a husband and wife who actually love each other! What excellent role models you and Eileen would make—forty-five years together!

If you're getting the brush-off from the Children's Church director, consider volunteering for some of the "extras" in Children's Church: making cookies, designing bulletin boards, duplicating handouts, visiting absentees, etc. Once you've proven just how much "senior citizens" are capable of doing, I think you'll become a regular part of the teaching staff.

Are you too old? Don't believe it for a moment!

Andy

8.

ADDITIONAL COMPONENTS OF THE CHILDREN'S CHURCH PROGRAM

The entire Children's Church program for a particular Sunday should be built around one specific teaching aim. The Bible lesson is developed around this aim, introducing, explaining, illustrating and applying it. A Bible lesson without a specific teaching aim usually goes nowhere. It tends to wander and meander with no specific focus and is very ineffective. It is crucial that our Bible lesson be structured around a central teaching aim that is brief enough to be remembered, clear enough to be written down, and specific enough to be achieved.

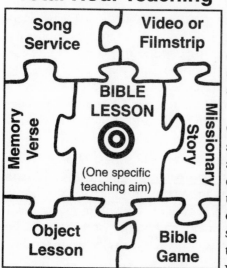

The various other parts of the Children's Church hour must also support and reinforce the teaching aim. Each component of the entire teaching period should be tied to that one central aim, developing and reemphasizing it. The song service, the memory verse, the puppet show, the filmstrip or video, and the missionary story should all fit together to teach and reteach the teaching aim for the day.

How many Children's Churches I've observed that don't follow this principle! The memory verse teaches trust in God, while the lesson stresses obedience to parents. The puppets present a skit on witnessing, and the video for the day teaches creation! It's almost like handing the student several jigsaw puzzle pieces, each from a different puzzle, then expecting him to be able to fit them all together!

The most effective teaching situation is one in which all the components of Children's Church tie together around one teaching aim, each part reinforcing and reemphasizing one particular biblical truth until the student cannot miss it.

Let's take a look at some of the various components of the Children's Church service that we have not yet discussed, and consider the ways to use them most effectively.

THE SONG SERVICE

Music is an integral part of any Children's Church service, and its importance should never be minimized. Most children love to sing. A lively, cheerful song service not only offers praise to God; it also creates a bright, enjoyable atmosphere in the service and sets the stage for effective learning.

The song leader should be a lively, energetic person who enjoys music and believes that when kids sing, they should SING! He should be full of pep and enthusiasm. The song leader who never smiles or shows enthusiasm and looks as if he could use a good, stiff dose of Geritol will never lead a cheerful, heartwarming song service. (If you lead the singing in Children's Church and you are not an energetic, lively person by nature, ask God to give you the zip and enthusiasm you lack. He can do it!)

Pace the song service. As you select your songs, choose lively, enthusiastic songs and choruses for the opening segment of Children's Church. Action songs with motions are very appropriate here. Choose songs that the children enjoy singing, selections that will motivate them to sing heartily. Have the students stand for the first song or two, be seated for the next, etc. Make this part of the service as lively and enthusiastic as you can.

The second portion of the song service (scheduled after the memory verse on the sample schedule in Chapter 2) should also involve energetic singing, with lots of action choruses and motions. Again, have the pupils stand on some songs; allow them to remain seated on others.

The songs just before the lesson time should be of a quieter nature, slower and calmer in style. Use the songs to settle the students, preparing them to listen to the Bible message.

130

It's appropriate to have the students stand for a song or two at this point, but avoid the noisy, energetic type of song. The last song before the lesson should be a very quiet, slow song such as "God Is So Good." A quiet song can have a calming effect upon the entire group, settling them in preparation for the lesson. The alert song leader can avoid many discipline problems simply by choosing the appropriate songs for the various parts of the program.

Select the songs carefully. Always remember that the song service is more than just a time-filler. The songs you choose for your Children's Church students to sing should accomplish one or more of the three objectives: evangelism, teaching and worship. But the wrong song may not accomplish any objective, so be selective.

A good song service starts with well-chosen songs. Look for songs with:

Simple words. Check the lyrics of the songs you use to ascertain that the words mean what they say and say what they mean, especially to Primaries and Juniors. Choose songs that communicate the truth in a way that children can grasp it. The message of the song is lost to your students if they don't understand the words.

The song says that Jesus wants me for a sunbeam. What in the world does that mean?

Correct doctrine. Examine your songs carefully to make sure that they are doctrinally correct. Occasionally you'll find a song or a hymn—even in the church hymnal—that is poorly worded or teaches incorrect doctrine. Don't use it.

A message that reinforces the teaching aim. Again, remember that the songs you choose should teach the same truth as the Bible lesson. Your songs should dovetail with the day's teaching aim. It's not always possible to select songs for the entire service that are "on target," but as often as you can, choose the songs that reinforce the aim for a most effective teaching hour.

Appropriate style. While the music for Children's Church can be cheerful and lively, it must be sacred. Avoid the worldly styles that are becoming increasingly popular in today's music for children.

Use visualized songs and choruses. There are a number of publishers that produce a variety of outstanding visualized children's songs. Colorful flashcards and books with large text and cheerful illustrations add impact to your song service. Songs that are visualized are more meaningful to the students, and the new pupil can join right in the singing, even though he may not know the words. An added benefit of using visualized songs is that you can use kid volunteers to help hold the visuals.

If you can't find a visual for a particular song, consider visualizing it yourself. Print the lyrics in large, block letters on full sheets of posterboard, then paste colorful pictures or drawings beside the text to illustrate the message. Or you can use your computer to produce some first-class visualized songs on overhead transparencies. (Believe it or not, you need to obtain permission from the copyright holders before visualizing the lyrics for your class.)

Explain the meaning of the song. Many times an otherwise excellent song may have a word or phrase that needs explanation. If an obscure term or line in the song can be clarified with a brief definition or explanation, go ahead and use the song, especially if it reinforces your teaching theme for the day. Almost any song becomes more meaningful if you occasionally discuss it before singing it.

The song about the wise and foolish builders has an excellent message, but many Primaries and Juniors entirely miss the meaning unless the teacher introduces it with a simple explanation from Matthew 7. If the Children's Church lesson teaches the importance of obedience to the Scriptures, being "doers of the word," this song would be

Joey sez:
"I like to sing about the Lord Jesus! The songs remind us that He loves us."

an excellent choice for the song service, but be sure to discuss the meaning briefly so that your students don't miss the message.

> # An effective song service:
> 1. **Pace the song service.**
> 2. **Select songs carefully:**
>   a. **Simple words**
>   b. **Correct doctrine**
>   c. **Emphasis on aim**
>   d. **Appropriate style**
> 3. **Use visualized songs & choruses.**
> 4. **Explain the meaning.**

THE MEMORY VERSE

Your Primaries and Juniors are at the ideal age for memorizing—it will never be easier than right now—and Bible memorization should be  a part of your Children's Church ministry. Many teachers (both Sunday school and Children's Church) attempt to "assign" a different memory verse every week. Very few of the students actually learn the verses, and it's easy to become discouraged and give up on Scripture memory.

Why not back off from attempting a new verse each week and work on just one verse a month? If you teach, drill, recite and review one verse for four weeks straight, almost every student who has regularly attended will know it without even trying! It's far better to teach twelve new verses each year and have your students really memorize and remember them, than to "teach" fifty-two verses that no one recalls at the end of the year.

Introduce the new verse on the first Sunday of the month with a short drill (five to seven minutes). Before Children's Church begins, write the verse out on a dry erase board or overhead transparency, with the reference before and after the text.

Matthew 6:33
But   ye first the kingdom
of God, and his
and   these things shall
be added   you.
Matthew 6:33

As you introduce the verse in class, read it aloud one time, explaining any new words or unfamiliar expressions. Then have the entire class read the verse aloud several times, including the reference. After reading the verse two or three times in unison, have the boys stand and read the verse, then the girls, then those students wearing red, then those wearing green or yellow, then those who are Chicago Bulls fans, etc.

The object is to have the class read the verse *aloud* several times. After reading the verse aloud six or eight times, begin erasing one or two words each time the verse is read, continuing until the entire verse is erased. Allow the students to choose the words to be erased, but inform them that you are choosing only those students who are reading the verse each time. You'll usually get one hundred percent participation!

Drill the verse for just a few minutes each Sunday for the first three weeks. Keep the drills short and exciting, visualizing the verse in a different way each week (overhead projector, dry erase board, flannel board, chalkboard, etc.).

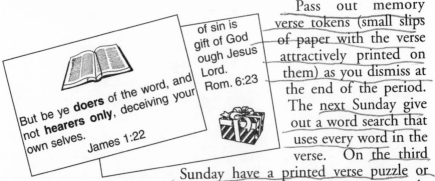

But be ye **doers** of the word, and not **hearers only**, deceiving your own selves. James 1:22

of sin is
gift of God
ough Jesus
Lord.
Rom. 6:23

Pass out memory verse tokens (small slips of paper with the verse attractively printed on them) as you dismiss at the end of the period. The next Sunday give out a word search that uses every word in the verse. On the third Sunday have a printed verse puzzle or quiz to hand out, etc. Handouts can be very effective in memory work.

On the fourth Sunday of the month, review the verse very briefly, then allow the kids who recite it to receive a small prize. In our Children's Church of 120 kids, we would take the boys to two other classrooms to recite their verse while the girls had a song service. All but one or two workers would go along to listen to the verses. As each boy said his verse (or failed to), he was dismissed back to the Children's Church room. When all the boys were finished, the girls would be dismissed to the reciting rooms. The entire process took only six to eight minutes, and approximately eighty percent of the students could quote the verse!

I strongly suggest using only the King James Version for memory work. Children memorize it easily, the translation is accurate, and it gives a uniformity to your memory work as a class.

Periodically review the previous verses for the year. Display them on bulletin boards or verse cards on the walls, plan special memory contests, and occasionally review them in your Bible games. Your Primaries and Juniors are fantastic memorizers, and that skill should be directed toward the Word!

> **Encouraging Bible Memorization:**
> 1. **Teach one verse each month.**
> 2. **Visualize the verse.**
> 3. **Drill each Sunday.**
> 4. **Use memory verse tokens.**
> 5. **Have a monthly contest.**
> 6. **Use the King James Version.**
> 7. **Review previous verses.**
> 8. **Memorize along with the students.**

THE MISSIONARY STORY

The missions emphasis is another vital aspect of a well-balanced children's ministry. Primaries and Juniors not only need to be aware of the need of people in other lands to hear the Gospel, but they also need to realize that they can have a part in the missionary outreach of their church.

This missions education can be accomplished in a number of ways (visiting missionaries, age-appropriate films, videos, or filmstrips, lessons on missions, etc.), but one of the most enjoyable of all is the missionary story.

Your local Christian bookstore should carry books of short, intriguing missions stories that an average storyteller can use to fascinate the students. A number of publishers produce colorful flashcards and visual books to visualize some of the more exciting tales from other lands.

You're after VARIETY in your Children's Church program, so don't use a missionary story every single week. Once a month is often enough, with an occasional four- or five-part continued story that runs for several weeks straight.

The missionary story presents an opportunity to enlist outside help, or perhaps you can utilize one of your workers who does not care to prepare a lesson every week. (Imagine the reactions of your students if your pastor were to pop in one Sunday with a ten-minute missionary story!)

Select an appropriate story (or continued story), then give it to your storyteller a month in advance. Be sure to select a person who will put some enthusiasm into the presentation and who understands that it is important to tell the story rather than to read it. Be sure to communicate your teaching aim so the story will fit in with the day's lesson.

VIDEOS, FILMSTRIPS AND MOVIES

Projected visuals can be very effective teaching media. A carefully selected video, filmstrip or movie can present a particular message with a powerful impact and make an impression that will last a lifetime.

I grew up in Sunday school and church and heard countless lessons and messages, many of which I've forgotten, but I remember the message of some of the films I saw thirty years ago! Videos and films can bring tremendous VARIETY to your teaching situation.

As you use projected visuals, be sure to observe the following guidelines:

Preview every film or video. Never show a film or video without previewing it. A friend of mine showed a secular film (from the public library) to his Junior High class without previewing it and got the shock of his life. The "color scale" on the leader of the film included a shot of a nude woman! You won't face that with Christian films, of course, but you can still be in for some big surprises, so be sure to preview every single item you show, no matter what the source. As you preview the films or videos, watch for:

Age appropriateness. Films and videos are usually targeted toward a particular age group. Hopefully you know your students well enough to recognize the films that are geared above or beneath their age group and will reject those in favor of the ones that will address their interests and needs.

Correct doctrine. As with other teaching materials, never assume that because it comes from a Christian source, the teaching will always be correct. Check it out first!

Proper philosophy, dress or music. Again, never assume. I've viewed "Christian" films that advocated or condoned deceit, selfishness, greed, etc. Remember the standards of the producer may not be the same as your own.

Same teaching aim. As we've already stated, any video or film you show in Children's Church should tie in with your teaching aim for that particular Sunday. Many materials today give a brief synopsis on the back cover, including the "theme" or aim.

Use films and videos to achieve VARIETY. Don't show a film or video every week. If you run across some outstanding videos that will enhance your teaching ministry, you might plan to show one a month.

A lengthier video—forty or fifty minutes—might be shown in three or four shorter segments, in much the same way as a continued missionary story.

Introduce the film. Prepare your students by asking a couple of key questions or mentioning some things they should watch for as they view the film. A good message or lesson deserves a proper introduction, and it's often the same with a film.

Discuss the film afterwards. Lead a brief discussion immediately after the viewing. A few key questions can help the teacher evaluate the impact of the presentation and reinforce the message that the students received. Keep the discussion brief.

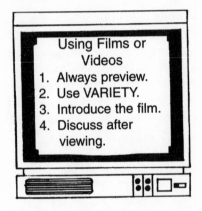

Using Films or Videos
1. Always preview.
2. Use VARIETY.
3. Introduce the film.
4. Discuss after viewing.

USING PUPPETS

Puppets can bring VARIETY and fun to Children's Church, and they can be used as effective teaching tools. One word of caution: most of today's children have seen more puppet shows than you can imagine, and it takes a first-class puppet presentation to hold their attention very long.

When using puppets, be certain that you have well-written scripts that will address the interests of your students, that your puppeteers practice and practice until their skills and timing are flawless, and that the end result is a quality presentation. Today's children are quickly bored with a second-rate puppet presentation.

138

As with the other components of Children's Church, be sure to select skits that match your teaching aim. This must be done far enough in advance to allow your puppet troupe adequate time to practice.

Don't use puppets every Sunday. Again, use VARIETY. Once a month is usually enough, even with the best of the best operating the puppets. Puppets can be very enjoyable if used correctly, but be sure not to overuse them.

Another note of caution: always remember that puppets are make-believe characters. Don't have them pray to receive Jesus as Saviour during a puppet skit. This places the act of receiving Christ into the realm of fantasy for many children. The kids know that the puppets are not real characters; therefore, they assume that perhaps getting saved isn't real either.

Use your puppets to teach character traits such as honesty, obedience, loyalty, etc., but remember that puppets are not the best medium for presenting the gospel message and the plan of salvation.

This chapter dealt briefly with five different teaching methods: music, Scripture memory, missionary stories, films or videos, and puppets. Space does not permit a thorough treatment of these components of your ministry; our objective was to discuss the integration of these into your Children's Church program. Further reading is suggested.

1 Used by permission of Child Evangelism Fellowship, P.O. Box 348, Warrenton, MO 63383

2 Used by permission of Child Evangelism Fellowship, P.O. Box 348, Warrenton, MO 63383

Evaluating the Song Service

YES NO

___ ___ 1. Was the song leader energetic? friendly? enthusiastic?

___ ___ 2. Was the song service cheerful and up-lifting?

___ ___ 3. Did it create an atmosphere of warmth, love and worship?

___ ___ 4. Were the songs visualized?

___ ___ 5. Were the visuals large enough for all to see?

___ ___ 6. Were the songs carefully selected?

___ ___ 7. Were the words of the songs easily under-stood?

___ ___ 8. Did they need explanation?

___ ___ 9. Did the songs teach correct doctrine?

___ ___ 10. Did the songs tie in with the day's teaching aim?

___ ___ 11. Did the song leader pace the song service, using active songs with motions at the beginning of the hour and quieter, calmer songs just before the lesson?

___ ___ 12. Was the accompanist provided with sheet music before the service began?

___ ___ 13. Did the children enjoy singing?

___ ___ 14. Did the song service help accomplish the objectives of the Children's Church hour: evangelism, teaching and worship?

Checking Our Memory Work

YES NO

___ ___ 1. Do we teach one verse each month?

___ ___ 2. Are the memory verse drills exciting?

___ ___ 3. Do I memorize the verses?

___ ___ 4. Do my workers memorize the verses?

___ ___ 5. Do I visualize the verse for each drill?

___ ___ 6. Do I use a VARIETY of visuals?

___ ___ 7. Do we send attractive memory verse tokens home with the students?

___ ___ 8. Do we have a monthly contest?

___ ___ 9. Do we regularly review previous verses?

Video

Evaluating a Film or Video Presentation

YES NO

___ ___ 1. Did I preview the film or video before showing it?

___ ___ 2. Was the video geared toward the age group of my students?

___ ___ 3. Was it the right length for this service?

___ ___ 4. Did it tie in with my teaching aim for the day?

___ ___ 5. Did the video teach correct doctrine and biblical philosophy?

___ ___ 6. Did I introduce the film or video properly to prepare the students for the viewing?

___ ___ 7. Was the screen or monitor positioned so that every student could see it clearly?

___ ___ 8. Was the volume set at the right level?

___ ___ 9. Did I plan discussion questions to use after the viewing?

___ ___ 10. Did the film or video enhance my teaching?

Taking a Second Look—
Our Use of Puppets

YES NO

___ ___ 1. Do we use puppets for VARIETY in our program, rather than using them every week?

___ ___ 2. Is the puppet stage bright and attractive?

___ ___ 3. Is it high enough for all to see?

___ ___ 4. Are the puppets clean and in good repair?

___ ___ 5. Do the puppet skits tie in with the day's
teaching aim?

___ ___ 6. Are the skits appropriate for our age
group?

___ ___ 7. Do the skits hold the interest of the students?

___ ___ 8. Are the skits brief and fast-moving?

___ ___ 9. Do we refrain from having a puppet
"receive Christ," realizing that children
often have trouble separating make-
believe from reality?

___ ___ 10. Do the puppeteers practice regularly?

___ ___ 11. Do they present a quality program?

___ ___ 12. Is the mouth action of each puppet in perfect sync with the words of the dialogue or
song?

___ ___ 13. Do the puppets seem to make "eye contact" with each other and with the audience?

___ ___ 14. Are the puppets' movements realistic and
lifelike?

___ ___ 15. Have the puppets developed personali-
ties?

___ ___ 16. Do we get a positive response from the
students when the puppets make their
appearance?

Ask Andy!

Dear Andy,

As a junior-age student I used to enjoy Sword drills in class, but we've just about given up on them in Children's Church. When one kid finds the verse and starts reading it, the rest of the group goes haywire, slapping their Bibles shut, talking, etc. Nobody even listens to the verse!

I know it's good practice in finding Scripture passages, but why take the time to read the verse if the kids aren't even going to listen? Any suggestions?

Abby Westminster

Dear Abby,

Who ever would have thought that I'd be giving advice to "Dear Abby"?

My workers and I have faced the same problem for years, and I never knew what to do about it. A pastor's wife in Pennsylvania showed me the solution, and it's so simple I'm embarrassed that I didn't think of it!

This dear lady gave one point to the team of the kid who found the verse first, then gave a point to the kid who could answer a question (from the verse). As soon as one kid found the verse and started reading, the rest of the class immediately got quiet and listened intently to the verse, knowing that a question was to follow!

Is that a great solution or what? I just wish I could say that it was my idea!

Andy

Dear Andy,

We have about thirty kids in Children's Church, but things are pretty dead. The singing is pathetic, and we can't get the kids to participate for anything! Any suggestions?

Jim Shortz

Dear Jim,

Start using Bible review games! I don't even need to inquire as to whether or not you use them, since no teacher who uses Bible games ever has your complaint.

Once you get started on Bible games, participation in your class will blossom like dandelions after a spring rain.

Andy

Dear Andy,

I lead the singing in our Children's Church, but I'm just not the enthusiastic type. By nature I'm a quiet, laid-back sort of person, and it's hard for me to act like I'm excited and full of enthusiasm. Can you help?

Sally Forth

Dear Sally,

Good news! Quiet, laid-back sort of people can learn to be energetic and enthusiastic!

Ask the Lord to give you the enthusiasm you need, and then just act as if you have it. If you lead songs for forty children, pretend that you're in front of five hundred!

Project your voice, make your gestures and expressions BIG, and give it all you've got! After awhile, it'll come naturally. The Lord will help.

By nature I'm a quiet, laid-back sort of person myself, but with the Lord's help I can walk into an auditorium or gymnasium and grab the attention of a thousand kids.

People always tell me, "You have so much energy!"

If only they knew!
For the children,

Andy

Dear Andy,

I direct our Children's Church program. My song leader is a young man with good musical ability, tons of enthusiasm, and a dynamic personality.

The problem is, we can't depend on him. Half the time he's late for Children's Church, and the other half he doesn't even show, so I have to get someone else. He doesn't even bother to call!

Should I try to replace him?

Marshall Artz

Dear Marshall,

As someone once said, "The greatest ability is dependability." An unfaithful worker is usually a liability rather than an asset. Remember that your workers are role models for your students.

Make an appointment to visit this man in his home, and discuss the matter with him. Don't pull any punches. Let him know that you need workers who can be counted on, and ask if he is willing to commit himself to punctuality and faithfulness in order to serve in Children's Church. If he is unable or unwilling, kindly inform him that you must replace him.

Andy

Dear Andy,

I've noticed that when the Beginner Church children take their bathroom break, a teenage girl takes the little boys to the bathroom. Is this appropriate?

Max Wellhouse

Dear Max,

We're finally learning that sex offenders come in both genders, all ages and even from "good" homes. No, I don't think the situation you described is appropriate.

You're safest to have women or teenage girls assist the little girls, and men or teenage boys assist the little boys. In today's society, you can't be too careful.

Incidentally, your church would do well to do a background check on every worker who will have contact with children, from the nursery through the youth department. Again, we can't be too careful.

For the children,

Andy

9.

CHILDREN'S CHURCH VISITATION

The ministry of Children's Church extends far beyond the sixty or eighty minutes that the teacher spends with his Primaries and/or Juniors in the classroom on Sunday morning. An effective teacher is deeply involved in the lives of his students. The teacher who knows each of his students by name, understands their needs, their fears, their likes and dislikes, and is intimately familiar with their personal interests will impact the students for Christ. This teacher prays daily for his students. He spends time with them, both in class and outside of class. You'll often find him visiting in the homes of his young students.

Visitation is a vital part of any effective Children's Church ministry. By visiting in the home, the teacher gets to know the student, acquaints himself with the student's family, and gets an inside look into the home-life. The teacher who visits in the home shows the student and his family that he cares for that young person as an individual. He has an opportunity to acquaint the parents with the ministry of Children's Church. If the parents are unsaved or unchurched, he has an excellent opportunity to present Christ, as well as extend a personal invitation to take advantage of the church's ministry to adults.

I have never met a teacher with a warm, personal relationship with his students who did not make a regular habit of visiting in the pupils' homes.

Cindy sez:
"I love it when Mrs. Thomas comes to see me. She's a really neat teacher!"

There are various types or phases of Children's Church visitation. Let's take a brief look at each.

New Prospect Visitation

An alert teacher who has a heart for reaching young souls is always on the lookout for new prospects for his class. This teacher usually has a pocket or purse full of gospel tracts or church brochures. He's quick to notice a Junior or Primary child at the grocery store, the library, or the gas station, and never misses an opportunity to offer a discreet, polite invitation to the child and his parents.

He also plans specific times of new-prospect visitation. When another church member mentions that a family with children has moved into his neighborhood, he soon makes an appearance, introducing his Children's Church ministry to the new family, and issuing a warm invitation to attend. When he becomes aware of a large population of school-age youngsters in a nearby apartment building or subdivision, he plans a canvassing project.

As you visit for new prospects for Children's Church, always keep the following in mind:

Dress neatly but casually. Years ago it was imperative that the church visitation team be dressed in Sunday suit and tie. People expected the "church people" to be well-dressed. But in today's society, the person who is neat, well-groomed but casual is often received better than the over-dressed visitor.

Always be polite and courteous. Remember that you are an uninvited trespasser. Don't allow this thought to intimidate you, but do use it as a reminder always to put your best foot forward while on visitation. Be careful to use sidewalks rather than cut across people's lawns. Respect "day-sleeper" signs. Approach the house or apartment with a smile on your face, and be warm, cheerful and friendly as you explain the purpose of your visit.

Introduce yourself, your church, and your Children's Church ministry. Get to the point of your visit as quickly as possible. Some people are ill at ease when you mention the name of your church but will relax as soon as you begin describing your ministry to the children. Perhaps they are intimidated by the prospect of a hard-sell invitation to your church and are put at ease when they realize that your main interest lies in acquainting them with your ministry for their children. As quickly as possible, explain your reason for being on their doorstep.

Use quality printed materials. An attractive church tract or brochure  helps establish your credibility. The subject of your visit unconsciously recognizes that you are who you say you are, and a barrier of suspicion begins to melt away. Politely hand your printed material to the adult at the door as you make your introduction.

If a child is present, use an attention-getter. Remember, you are a total stranger to both the parent and the child, and they are under no obligation to listen to anything you have to say. Carry a magic trick or two in your pocket and use them as you make friends with the child and his parents.

 I have found that balloon sculptures are the best door-openers you can possibly imagine. I carry a pocketful of the skinny balloons used to make animals, hats, etc. The shyest youngster becomes interested when you start making a balloon dog or teddy bear on his doorstep. The most hostile adult warms to you as you hand her child a balloon creation. Learn to use simple attention-getters to establish rapport with the family as you visit.

Keep your visit brief. Again, remember that you are an uninvited guest and are possibly interrupting a busy schedule, even if the people are too polite to say so. State your business and extend your invitation, giving as much information as possible, then prepare to move on. Unless the occupants obviously want you to stay longer, be careful not to stay too long and wear out your welcome. Sometimes the briefest visits are the most effective ones.

Visitor Follow-Up Visitation

The alert Children's Church leader makes a point to visit in the homes of the kids who have come to Children's Church for the first time. This home visit should take place as soon as possible after the Sunday that the visitor attended. The object of this visit is to get to know the child and his family, to ascertain whether or not they know the Lord as Saviour, to introduce the ministry of the church and more especially the Children's Church, and to answer any questions.

Begin the visit by introducing yourself and expressing your appreciation for the child's attendance in Children's Church. Ask a few questions to get to know the family, and be sure to welcome them to the community if they are new. Share a little of your background: family, job situation, ministries in the church, etc. Then describe your Children's Church ministry, answering any questions that the family may have.

A useful tool for this type visitation is a Children's Church scrapbook. From time to time have a shutterbug in your church take pictures  of the various aspects of your Children's Church service, being sure to include shots of your puppets in action, Bible games, behavior contests, lesson visuals, etc., so the family gets a feel for the tremendous VARIETY of teaching media and methods that you employ. Mount these in an attractive format in a scrapbook or ring binder. Include interesting shots of the group of kids, and catch some of your workers in various aspects of ministry. Don't forget to record your Children's Church outings on film as well, and be sure that they find a place in the scrapbook.

During your visit, inform the child and his family of any upcoming Children's Church activities or outings. Extend a personal invitation for the child to participate, and leave a flier or announcement as a reminder of the date and time.

As with new-prospect visitation, be brief. Don't be in a hurry to leave, but do be alert and make sure that you don't overstay your welcome. Conclude the visit by thanking the child and family for visiting Children's Church and expressing a desire to see the child return.

Absentee Visitation

What an important part of our ministry, and yet, how often we neglect it! Any of our regulars who start to miss should automatically receive a visit from us or from one of our workers.

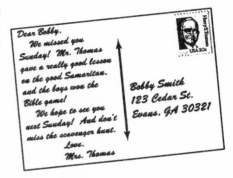

Dear Bobby,
We missed you Sunday! Mr. Thomas gave a really good lesson on the good Samaritan, and the boys won the Bible game!
We hope to see you next Sunday! And don't miss the scavenger hunt.
Love,
Mrs. Thomas

Bobby Smith
123 Cedar St.
Evans, GA 30321

Keep good attendance records on all your students. When a student misses a Sunday or two, be sure to mail a card or make a phone call to let him know that you noticed his absence and that he is important to you. If the student fails to attend on the next Sunday, plan a visit in the home that very next week.

When you learn that one of your students has an extended illness or is in the hospital, a friendly visit from you and some of your workers is definitely in order. Take along a small gift such as a game or puzzle or a good book.

During the visit share bits of information from the Children's Church service—which team won the Bible game, an update on team points for an attendance contest, etc. Leave a copy of any handouts, Bible-reading slips, etc., that were passed out to the students at the conclusion of the Children's Church service.

Salvation Follow-Up Visitation

Any child making a salvation decision in Children's Church should immediately receive a follow-up visit. The objective of this visit is to inform the parents of the child's spiritual decision, to review the decision with the child (to make certain that he fully understands), and to answer any questions that the child may have.

Make use of printed material. There are some excellent salvation tracts available for children, as well as some first-class salvation follow-up materials. Leave both of these with the child and his parents. The salvation tracts can be a good review to help the child think through his decision to receive Christ as Saviour, and the follow-up booklets can be a

New Life For Boys & Girls

helpful source of information and instruction to encourage him in his new Christian life.

Discuss baptism with the child and his parents. If the child understands the meaning of baptism and seems ready and willing, seek parental permission during this visit. If the child does not seem to understand the purpose and meaning of this ordinance, do not press the issue at this time.

Children's Church visitation is often most effective when you have a partner. Enlist one of the other Children's Church workers to accompany you. The presence of a friend can be an encouragement as you make your visits (especially when you step onto a porch to come face-to-face with a horse-sized Doberman pinscher!).

Use some of your faithful Juniors as visitation partners! This not only gets the child involved in ministry, but you get a better reception from the people you are visiting, both children and adults. Strangers trust you more quickly when you have children accompanying you on your visits. If you are the only adult, be certain that you have at least two children accompanying you at all times so that your motives are never under suspicion. The very best and safest situation, of course, is always to have another adult, preferably your spouse, with you and the children.

Visitation can be a lot of work, and it can require a sizable amount of time. But it can also produce tremendous results. Any Children's Church leader who desires an effective ministry to children will recognize the importance of this aspect of ministry.

The work load can be shared. If you have a staff of workers serving with you, encourage them to take some visitation assignments to help lighten your load. Be sure to keep accurate records so you know that the visits are being made and so you are kept aware of any follow-up visits that need to be made.

Visitation is a vital part of any well-rounded children's ministry, and this is especially true of Children's Church. Only by visiting your students in their homes will you fully understand your students' backgrounds, recognize their needs, and be prepared to assist them in their spiritual growth.

Dear Andy,

I thoroughly enjoy working in Children's Church, but one thing that really discourages me is the rapid turnover of the kids to whom we minister. A lot of the kids come for just a few weeks, then stop coming for one reason or another. Isn't there something we can do?

Della Ware

Dear Della,

Yes, there is something you can do. Dropouts can be a real discouragement to any teacher, but there are some ways to develop faithfulness among your students.

Pray. Pray daily for your students. Prayer is one of the most important aspects of your ministry.

Prepare. Many times kids drop out of church just because we have not taken the time to prepare a quality program. Kids figure it this way: If Children's Church is boring or does not meet my needs, why go?

Visit. Show these kids that you care by following up on them. You and your staff should work together to go after all absentees before you lose them completely.

It takes work, but it's worth it!

Andy

Dear Andy,

In our Children's Church we have a lot more girls than boys (about a 3-to-1 ratio). Anytime we have a contest with the boys against the girls, the boys give up quickly with the complaint, "There's more girls." Any suggestions?

Lou Slips

Dear Lou,

Start by seating the boys and girls together rather than placing the boys on one side and girls on the other. The gender imbalance won't be quite so obvious.

If you use contests in which the numerical disadvantage creates a serious handicap (attendance contests, offering contests, etc.), consider dividing teams by grade. In competition where numbers don't matter (Bible review games, Sword drills, etc.), you may wish to continue boys vs. girls.

If your staff is all female, pray and work to enlist some men teachers. (I've never yet seen an outstanding Children's Church ministry that employed just women teachers or just men teachers. The ideal is to use both.)

In some churches, the girls simply outnumber the boys. In others, the boys enjoy an overwhelming majority. Either way, there's not a whole lot you can do about it. Minister to the ones the Lord gives you!

Andy

Dear Andy,

One of the workers in my Children's Church is an elderly lady who taught school in Brooklyn for over forty years. The problem is, she is very rough—almost abusive—with the kids. If she sees a child misbehaving, she'll march up and grab an arm, jerk the kid out of his seat, and march the child back to sit with her, pinching the arm the whole while.

Most of our kids are afraid of her. Hardly a Sunday goes by but what she has one or more kids in tears.

How do I approach her and tell her to back off? Her treatment of the kids is inappropriate, but if I say anything, she's likely to bite my head off. Any help you can give would be appreciated.

R. U. Serious

Dear R. U.,

It sounds as if the kids are not the only ones who are afraid of this old saint! How do you approach her? ASAP! This Sunday! Before Children's Church starts!

Or better yet, take your pastor or another worker with you and visit this dear lady in her home. Lay the matter before her—this is no time to be timid—and let her know in no uncertain terms that this type of conduct cannot be tolerated. If she gets upset and resigns, you have lost nothing.

There is never any reason for a worker to abuse a student, physically or verbally. We need to be firm with the students and let them know that we are in charge, but there is never an occasion to be rough, harsh or hateful.

Deal with the situation *this week*!

Andy

P.S. I'm just glad it's you and not me!

Dear Andy,

We use behavior awards in Children's Church and reward the quietest kids. It's been very effective.

But how do I keep the workers quiet? On a typical Sunday morning most of the workers cluster in the back of the room— discussing the cost of groceries, Sally's new baby, or who had the latest operation. Sometimes they're louder than the teacher! And it's not just the women—the men are just as bad. Needless to say, it's been a real distraction.

I've mentioned the problem a couple of times, but nobody seems to pay any attention. What can I do?

Anna Conda

Dear Anna,

Seat the workers among the kids—that's where they should be anyway. It's always more effective to have the workers seated among the kids, singing, participating, and watching for little discipline problems, than to have them standing along the sides or back of the room.

The workers are usually taller than the kids and can create a visual barrier for the students behind them, so position them toward the ends of the rows. The back row, of course, will not have this problem, so the workers can be seated anywhere.

You might even want to mark seats in advance for the workers, positioning them in such a way that they do not obstruct any students' view, yet are placed at strategic points throughout the group.

In your workers' meetings, stress the need for constant prayer during the Children's Church service. A praying worker is not a talking worker.

Andy

10.
CHILDREN'S CHURCH OUTINGS

The early October days were crisp and cool but not yet cold. Piles of brilliant orange pumpkins were beginning to appear at roadside stands, and the hillsides were dazzling displays of fiery red, deep orange, and shimmering gold. Fall colors were nearly at their peak—perfect time for a hayride.

I called a local riding stable. "How much for a hayride? We'll bring seventy or eighty elementary children."

"Five dollars a head," was the reply.

I was shocked. (This was 1980.) "Five dollars?" I echoed. "But these are kids. And it's a large group! Can't you give us some kind of a break?"

"Five dollars per person. Doesn't matter how old they are."

After scouting around for a few days, I found a hunting preserve about thirty miles from the church. The man who ran it had a farm tractor and a couple of large hay wagons. And he was willing to mess with kids.

"How much?" I hesitantly asked.

"Just give me enough for gas for my tractor," he replied.

I charged the kids $2.00 a head, planning to give the tractor man one of the dollars and use the other to buy hot dogs, Cokes, chips, and snack cakes.

Friday evening we piled into two buses about an hour before sunset and drove toward the hunting preserve. The fall colors were superb, and

the workers and kids alike enjoyed the drive. We sang awhile, talked awhile, and just enjoyed being together.

When we reached our destination, I found that our host was prepared for us. Two farm wagons heaped with fresh hay were hitched behind an ancient red tractor. Wood was piled in the shape of a teepee in preparation for our bonfire, and there were even coat hangers for our hot dog roast! One glance at the man's preparations, and I knew we were in for a good evening.

The kids were clamoring to get off the buses, but an idea popped into my head, so I made them sit down again.

"The wagon closest to the tractor is the non-throwing wagon," I announced. "If you don't want to be in a hay fight, get on the first wagon. And the second wagon is the throwing wagon. If you're planning to throw hay or to try to stuff it down a leader's shirt, get on the second wagon.

"Now if you get on the first wagon, don't you dare throw hay or try to stuff it down someone's shirt. But if you're on the second wagon, don't you dare complain if someone throws hay or tries to stuff it down your shirt! Ready? Choose your wagon, and let's go have some fun!"

The kids and leaders piled onto the wagons, and the tractor took us on a pleasant hour's ride down a narrow lane through the forest. We must have scared every wild creature out of the woods with our shouts and laughter! By the time we returned to the bonfire area, the "throwing" wagon was nearly empty of hay!

The outing was a smashing success, and the hayride became an annual event. Teachers and students alike looked forward to it with eager anticipation. ("Hey, Mrs. Groover, are you going to ride the throwing wagon this year?")

Outings and activities are a vital part of any children's ministry. This is especially true of Children's Church. The teacher who sees his ministry as beginning when he walks in the door on Sunday morning and ending as he walks out, is missing it entirely!

If you want to impact kids for Christ, you've got to be involved in their lives outside the classroom setting.

Children's Church outings help the teacher establish rapport with the students. Outings help build relationships. They help the teacher

Joey sez:

"**Last Friday night was the best time in my whole life! Mr. Thomas took us camping! I got poison ivy, and Jeremy fell in the lake, but it was a lot of fun. Mr. Thomas does awesome bird calls. We didn't recognize what birds he was doing, so he told us. He can do a yellow-tailed woodpecker, a Baltimore blackbird, and a Russian dove! It was awesome! I love camping, and I think Mr. Thomas is a really cool teacher!**"

get to know the students intimately, and they help the student see the teacher as a person rather than just a talking face that quotes Scripture and shares Bible stories.

Imagine the delight of your pupils when they see you in bib overalls rather than that stuffy pin-striped suit! Imagine the important bond that forms with your boys (and your girls) as they get you down on the hay wagon, attempting to fill the front of those overalls with prickly hay! When your students discover first-hand that you are one who can laugh and joke and maybe even horseplay with them on occasion, an important bond of respect and love begins to grow.

Kids are more ready to listen to your Bible message on Sunday when they discover on Saturday that you love the Lord, that you love them, and that you love to have a good time.

When you spend time with your students outside of class, you get to know them. As you talk and joke and interact with them, you can't help but discover their likes and dislikes, their fears, their needs. You learn where they are spiritually. As a result, your lessons begin to hit home. You're now "on target." You know the needs of your pupils, and your lessons are geared to meet those needs.

Plan a Children's Church outing every month or, at the very minimum, every other month. Outings do take work and planning, but they are well worth it. Every minute spent in preparation for outings, as well as the time spent with the kids, will pay tremendous dividends.

Allow the kids to help plan the outings, or at least choose what type of outing they prefer. Occasionally I'd bring a dry erase board into Children's Church and tell the kids, "We need to plan our outings for April and May. I want you to tell me what kind of outing you would like to have. After we list your ideas, we'll take a vote and see which idea is the most popular."

As the students shared their ideas, I'd list them on the board, eliminating the impossible ones (trip to Six Flags) and the un-Christian ones (rock concert), explaining why they were not suitable. Then we'd take a quick vote and announce our next outing. In this way, the kids were involved in the planning, and Children's Church was not "mine"; it became "theirs."

Many of today's Primaries and Juniors do not spend much time outdoors, but they quickly become hooked on outdoor activities once they get a taste. Some of our favorite Children's Church outings were hayrides, cave explorations, hikes and canoe trips.

It's hard to describe the fun and fellowship that students and teachers can enjoy together in the great outdoors!

An outing that quickly became an annual favorite was the cave trip. One of my workers told me of a wild cave half an hour from the church. He and I made several explorations until we were thoroughly familiar with the layout. Once I knew the cave, we began taking groups of our students.

We limited the size of each group to twenty kids and took ten adults along, assigning two kids to each adult. On each trip we spent

approximately two hours exploring the cave, including a brief candle-light service three hundred feet underground!

As we rode the church bus back home, the kids munched on snacks (you can expend a lot of energy crawling through a cave), while the leaders were busy choosing four kids to receive special cave awards to be presented the next day in Children's Church.

The "dirty sock award" went to the kid with the muddiest clothes, while the "clean sock award" went to the kid with the cleanest. (You wouldn't believe how dirty some kids could get and how perfectly clean other kids could keep themselves!) The "dirty face award" was presented to the student with the muddiest face, hands and hair, while the student who stayed the cleanest received the "clean face award."

Memories of those cave trips are still special. Teachers and kids alike had fun that they will remember for a lifetime. Special teacher/student relationships were formed, and the impact of our Children's Church ministry was greatly enhanced as a result of our times together.

I remember one fourth-grade girl who was very distant the first two or three months she was in Children's Church. She was always cold and aloof, and we wondered if we were getting through to her at all.

She went on one of our cave trips and was terrified as we entered the cave. She clung to me during the entire outing, and I did my best to encourage and reassure her.

From that day forward, she was one of my biggest fans and became one of the most responsive kids in class! The Lord used the cave trip to draw her out of her shell, and we saw tremendous spiritual growth.

As you plan outings and activities for your Children's Church kids, be sure to observe the following guidelines:

Involve the students in planning. As we already mentioned, the kids thoroughly enjoy being in on the selection and planning process. You won't be able to use all of their ideas, of course, but your students will get a real thrill out of being able to have some input.

Announce the outings well in advance. Begin announcing your outing a month in advance during your Children's Church service. Distribute handouts describing the outing at the close of the service so the parents can get accurate information. Be sure to include all the details: date, starting and closing time, destination, cost (if any), appropriate clothing (one mother will send her daughter on a cave trip in a brand-new designer outfit), and any needed equipment (flashlight, spare batteries, etc.).

If the children need to bring a sack lunch or money for a stop at McDonald's, make certain that it's on the flier. The flier should tell the parents if they need to feed their children before they come or if you will provide a meal. Spell out every detail as clearly as you can. (And then you'll still get a dozen phone calls.)

Last but not least, be sure to specify what ages are invited, or some parent will send a three-year-old!

Enlist adult help. Your Children's Church teachers and staff are the ideal chaperones and helpers. The main objective of the outing is to establish rapport and build relationships with the students, so your workers will want to be involved, but don't just assume that they will. Get a commitment from each for that particular outing, and if you are short of help, enlist some church parents.

When we planned our cave trips, I limited the groups to twenty children (they signed up in advance, with parental permission slips), and I got commitments from ten adults to accompany us. There were a few scary spots in our cave, but with two children assigned to each adult, we never had the slightest accident.

Put the safety of the children first. I have two fiberglass canoes, and I've made over three hundred canoe trips with my Primaries and Juniors.

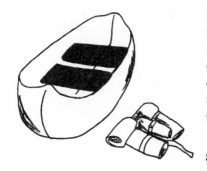

No child ever set foot in one of my canoes without a life vest (securely fastened and checked). And we did our canoeing on flat water, with no rapids or treacherous currents. I never took the slightest chance with the safety of the children.

If you're planning an outdoor activity, check out the location in advance. Just because you're going to have a picnic at a state park doesn't mean there's no danger involved. Check it out. There may be an eighty-foot cliff just beyond the picnic area and no warning signs posted. Those lovely rhododendrons just below the playground may conceal a river with a powerful current and steep banks. There's always the threat of poison oak or poison ivy, which kids never remember to watch for.

I'm certainly not trying to discourage you from outdoor trips, but I'm saying that you should know in advance what you're getting into.

On one cave trip our guide (my song leader) wanted to take the group out a second entrance which I had never seen. I hesitated, but when he assured me that it was perfectly safe for Primaries and Juniors, at last I consented.

It turned out to be a twenty-five-foot chimney climb! Even some of my older boys were in tears by the time we got out. No one was hurt, but we got back to church forty-five minutes late. Parents were worried and angry.

I had made a mistake that I will never repeat: I took someone else's word regarding the safety of a situation I had not checked out, when the safety of the children was *my* responsibility.

Go over the rules with the students before they get off the bus or van. If there is a danger area, let them know that it is off limits and that there will be a penalty for any violator. ("If we see you down at the lake without an adult, you will sit on the van for twenty minutes. Got it?")

165

Use only qualified drivers. This is no time for a teenager with two months' driving experience to be playing chauffeur. If you are taking a church bus, make sure that the driver has his CDL.

Have an alternative plan. If you are planning an outdoor activity, it just might get rained out—unless you live in Arizona. If bad weather threatens, don't cancel the outing; be ready with Plan B. A scavenger hunt won't be any fun at all in the rain, so why not substitute a cartoon night, with popcorn and games?

Sometimes it's not the activity the kids are looking forward to as much as it is a chance to be with you. Don't disappoint them when the skating rink manager calls and cancels; be ready with Plan B.

Provide drinks and snacks. Most outings will involve more than just an hour or so, and a brief refreshment break is always welcome. The refreshments need not be elaborate—snack cakes and Kool-Aid, chips

and pretzels with Coke, or root beer floats. Many parents are more than willing to provide the refreshments for your outing if you just give them enough advance notice.

If you're planning a hike, cave trip, or other strenuous activity, be sure to take along plenty of water and Dixie cups, especially during the warm-weather months. Plan ahead; there may not be water available at your destination. (State and city parks are notorious for their non-working drinking fountains.)

Encourage visitors to come. When you announce your outings, encourage your students to invite their unchurched friends. Many times an outing can open the door to a family that would not have come to your church under any other circumstances. During the outing, present a brief (five- to ten-minute) devotional that includes the gospel plan.

Before I close this chapter, I must say this: if you planned a Children's Church outing three years ago and it was a total flop, please try again. Don't give up if your first attempt was a total failure. Make some notes on what went wrong, change some things, then try again. Your second outing will be an improvement, and your third one will be even better!

Children's Church outings are like just about everything else in life—you have to learn how to do them. A successful outing takes planning, workers, patience and flexibility. Some people have to make several attempts before they get the hang of it, but the end results are always worth the trouble. Your students will develop a loyalty and love for you that will warm your heart. Parents will occasionally express their appreciation, but the greatest results are in the classroom. Your teaching will be more effective than ever before!

Junior Church outings establish rapport and build relationships!

Guidelines for Outings:

1. Involve the students in planning.
2. Publicize the outing in advance.
3. Enlist adult help.
4. Put the safety of the children first.
5. Use only qualified drivers.
6. Have a bad-weather plan.
7. Provide drinks and snacks.
8. Encourage students to bring friends.
9. Enjoy the time together!

Favorite Outings and Activities

1. Hayrides (October)
2. Cave Trips (Anytime)
3. Picnics (April–October)
4. Scavenger Hunts (March–November)
5. Cartoon Nights (Winter)
6. Hikes (March–November)
7. Indoor Carnival (Winter)
8. Game Night (Nerf Ball Games, etc.) (Anytime)
9. Trail Rides (Spring or Fall)
10. Zoo Trips (Spring or Fall)
11. Kite-Flying Contests (March, April)
12. McDonald's Trip (Anytime)
13. Water Balloon Activities (Summer)
14. Miniature Golf (March–November)
15. Skating Parties (Anytime)
16. Canoe Trips (small groups) (May–October)

Planning the Outing

Date_____ Time_____   **Time of return**_____   Cost $_____
Estimated # of students_____
Destination_____
Description of activity _____
Drivers _____
Cars ___Van ___Bus (CDL) Church vehicles reserved ( )
Confirmed ( ) ___Accurate directions to location
Adult workers: confirmed one week in advance
_____( ) Phone # _____
_____( )   _____
_____( )   _____
_____( )   _____
_____( )   _____
_____( )   _____
Workers on standby:_____ Phone #_____
              _____   _____
              _____   _____

Fliers: # needed_____ Distribute:__/__/__
✔ Necessary info.: Description of activity:___Date:___Time:___Return: __
Cost:___Equipment needed:___Meal or snack details:___Age group invited:__
Appropriate clothing:___Permission slip:___
Meal or snack: (___Details covered on flier?)
___Children eat before coming.
___Children bring own lunch.
___Children bring money.
___Meal or snack provided by_____
___Serving utensils, individual tableware
___Water, clean-up supplies
Equipment needed for games or activity:

_____
_____
_____

Devotional planned by:_____ Topic? _____
Bad-weather alternative plan: _____
_____
_____

Ask Andy!

Dear Andy,

I'd like to plan more outings for our Children's Church kids, but most of our workers are on second shift and are just not available. Saturdays aren't much better.

Any suggestions?

Cindy Wrella

Dear Cindy,

Plan as many outings as you can with the entire Children's Church and staff. Enlist the help of church parents when you can't get enough workers.

You can also plan "mini-outings." Invite five or six students over to your house for a spaghetti supper, then play "hide-and-seek" in the backyard. Take several kids out to McDonald's (Dutch treat), then go window-shopping at the mall! Plan a "progressive dinner" with a few students. Have them each bring a few dollars, then visit the local fast-food boulevard, stopping at each restaurant and allowing each person to purchase only one small item at each stop! Invite several kids over to your house for a slumber party.

Small groups can be fun, and some good relationships can flourish. "Mini-outings" can be used to complement your regular Children's Church outings.

Andy

Dear Andy,

Our church runs three buses and a couple of vans, and we bring in quite a few children. The problem is, the church kids won't associate with the "bus kids." The "church kids" have their own little cliques, and so do the "bus kids."

We've taught on brotherly love and all that, but nothing seems to work. What can we do to break down this wall between the two groups?

Al Gebra

Dear Al,

Get these kids together at some time other than Sunday school or Children's Church. Plan some outings. There's something about an outing that forms bonds of love and camaraderie faster than anything else you could do.

Use outings and activities to "tear down the wall."

Andy

11.

HOW TO ENCOURAGE BIBLE READING

James 1:22 seems to sum up the objective of our Children's Church ministry in one concise command: "But be ye doers of the word, and not hearers only."

Isn't that what we're after as we teach the Word to our Primaries and Juniors—to guide them to be obedient to God as they learn His will from the Scriptures? The ultimate goal of our teaching is to lead our students to obey God's voice as revealed in His Word, the Bible.

When we teach on salvation, we're trying to lead the unsaved student to obey the Word and receive Jesus as Saviour. If the aim of the lesson is witnessing, we're attempting to show our students their responsibility to tell others about Christ, as revealed in the Bible. If we teach on honesty or obedience to authority or selflessness, etc., we're showing our students that these character traits are revealed in God's Word and that He desires these in our lives.

The ultimate purpose of the Bible lesson is to lead the student to obey the Word of God.

In order for the lesson to accomplish this, our application must be very specific, personal and practical. We must not only show the student what God wants him to do but also how to go about doing it. We must find tangible ways for our students to put our teaching into practice, to be "doers of the word, and not hearers only."

For example, we often teach on the importance of reading God's Word. We stress the need for each student to have a daily "quiet time," a time set aside for personal Bible reading and prayer. But do our students follow through on our teaching? How many of our Primaries and Juniors actually read the Bible during the week?

Several years ago I became determined to find out how many of my Children's Church kids were getting into God's Word on their own. I began to ask each week about their Bible-reading habits. The results were pretty discouraging. Fewer than ten percent of the group were reading on a regular basis, and we had taught on it so many, many times!

I began to search for a way to encourage my kids to get into God's Word faithfully during the week. What good was it to teach on the importance of daily Bible reading if my students weren't actually doing it?

It was discouraging to realize that my students were "hearers only," rather than "doers."

One week I prepared a list of references of seven short Scripture passages, labeling them Sunday, Monday, Tuesday . . . I duplicated 120 copies on the Spirit duplicator (that messy machine that produced those atrocious purple copies), then passed them out the next Sunday just before we dismissed. As I introduced the Bible-reading slips and explained their purpose, I told the students that I would be doing my Bible reading from these passages and that some of the leaders would as well.

We passed out Bible-reading slips the next several Sundays and began asking how many were actually doing the reading on a regular basis. To my delight, the number of faithful readers rose to somewhere between twenty and twenty-five percent of the group!

We began to prepare more attractive reading slips and continued passing them out weekly.

Another idea helped increase the number of faithful readers even further. One Sunday morning just before dismissing and passing out the Bible-reading slips, I held up several sheets of paper. "These sign-up sheets will be back on the table where you usually get your Bible-reading slips," I told the students. "If you'd like to get a phone call from one of the workers this week to check on your Bible reading, just put your name and phone number on one of the lists when you pick up your reading slip.

"One of us will try to call you at home one evening this week, but you won't know which evening we'll call. When we call, if you can honestly say that you have done your Bible reading that day, your name will go on a list, and you will receive a small prize next Sunday. It won't be anything big, but we just want to encourage you to read your Bible faithfully."

When we dismissed, the children flocked around the table, eager to sign up.

That was just the beginning. We continued the phone call system on a regular basis. The workers and I divided up the names so the phone calls wouldn't be too great a burden for one person. Some weeks we announced that there would be no prize for the Bible reading, but we would continue the phone calls. The kids signed up just as eagerly.

The bottom line of the phone call encouragement system was this: the number of faithful Bible readers rose almost immediately to over seventy percent!

We eventually dropped the prizes completely, but the number of readers didn't diminish a bit. The motivating factor was the personal attention we were giving the kids. We had not only taught about the importance of Bible reading, but we found a tangible way to get the kids into the Word, and we showed that we cared enough to check on them personally. The end result made the effort well worthwhile.

In the Bible-reading graph to the right, "A" represents the percentage of Junior Church students faithfully reading on their own. "B" represents the percentage faithfully reading with the encouragement of the Bible-reading slips, while "C" designates the percentage who read regularly with reading slips and phone call encouragement.

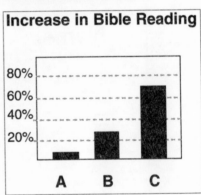

Increase in Bible Reading

Here's the thrust of this chapter in one concise statement: when you teach God's Word to Primaries and Juniors, find some tangible way to encourage your students to put your teaching into practice. Motivate them to integrate the Scripture into their everyday lives. The ultimate goal of Children's Church is to produce "doers of the word."

Before we leave this topic, allow me to mention a few guidelines to follow if you are interested in utilizing the Bible-reading slips or the phone call follow-ups:

1. Select short, simple passages. Many of your students are not proficient readers, so don't select long passages. Six or eight verses are ideal.

Sometimes we would choose topical passages that reinforced the teaching aim for that week or introduced the theme for the following week; at other times we read through one of the Gospels, a few verses at a time.

Daily Bible Reading
October 1–7

Front Page

2. Make the reading slip attractive. If you have access to a computer, use the greeting card function of a graphics program to design and print the reading slip. Using the church copier or the inexpensive copiers at a self-service print shop, duplicate the finished product on both sides of colored paper. Cut the sheets in half, fold them, and you have some very attractive Bible-reading slips.

3. Use children's artwork on the cover. We asked our students to submit artwork drawn in dark pencil or black ink, then we pasted it to the cover of the reading slip before duplicating it. We always included the name of the "artist."

The students thoroughly enjoyed seeing their work duplicated in this fashion, and we were never short of new artwork. It was just a personal touch, another way to tell the students that they were important to the Children's Church program.

4. Place a personal message inside. As the student opened the reading slip, he found the selected Scripture passages listed on the right-hand panel and a brief, cheerful message from one of the workers on the left-hand panel. This personal note stressed the importance of living for Jesus and reminded the student that he was loved at our church.

5. Use the back for announcements. Is the fall hayride coming up? Be sure to announce it on the back of the reading slip, giving date, time and cost. Include your home number for the parents who have questions. The back of the reading slip is also an excellent place to insert the memory verse for the month.

6. Check up the following Sunday. As we opened the Children's Church service, I would always ask, "How many of you have done your

Today is Mrs. Thomas' birthday! She won't tell us how old she is, but wish her a Happy Birthday anyway. Her number is 866-4341.

And don't miss the hayride! It's a week from Friday, and it's going to be fun. There'll be hot dogs and drinks, and a marshmallow roast. I'll see you on the throwing wagon!

Be faithful to read your Bible every day, and take time to talk to Jesus in prayer. He cares about you.

We're glad that you're a part of our Junior Church! We love you!

Mr. Ed

DAILY BIBLE READING

Sunday	-	John 1:1–7
Monday	-	John 1:8–14
Tuesday	-	John 1:15–23
Wednesday	-	John 1:24–30
Thursday	-	John 1:31–34
Friday	-	John 1:35–42
Saturday	-	John 1:43–51

Casting all your care upon him; for he careth for you.
I Peter 5:7

Inside Pages

Junior Church Hayride!

Friday, October 13
(5–9 p.m.)
Cost: $2.00

This year's hayride is going to be a blast! Don't miss it! Bring a friend and come have the time of your life! Mr. Groover is challenging Mr. Thomas to a championship hay fight!

Call 937-3798 for more information.

Back Page

Bible reading every day this week? How many of you forgot one day, but you did it six days? How many did it five. . . ?" This not only let us know how many of our students were getting into the Word, it also told the students that the Bible reading was a very important aspect of the Christian life.

We never belittled or embarrassed the children who did not participate in the Bible reading but encouraged them to get involved by continually giving out the reading slips and emphasizing the importance of the Scriptures.

If you are considering using the phone call follow-ups, follow these guidelines:

Sign-up must be voluntary. Most of our kids enjoyed the personal attention and were eager to sign up every Sunday, but there were always a few who chose not to sign up for one reason or another. The children who did not care to receive a phone call were never put on the spot or embarrassed in any way.

Make the calls early in the evening. We tried to place our calls between 6:00 and 8:00 p.m. This gave the child time to do his Bible reading after he got home from school, if that was his best time, but did not interfere with any child's bedtime.

Be polite and friendly. The purpose of the call is to encourage, never to berate, the student who had neglected his Bible reading. If a child told us, "I do my reading at night, and I haven't been able to do it yet," we would always ask, "Then did you do it last night?" An affirmative answer gave them credit for the reading.

To our surprise, most of our students seemed to be candid and honest when we called, and they would readily admit when they had forgotten their reading. We always took the child at his word when he gave an affirmative answer and never attempted to "quiz" him on the passage to ascertain that he was telling the truth.

The phone call follow-up system may not fit your ministry. You and your workers may not have the time to call your students every week, or you may not feel comfortable with such intimacy, but for our Children's Church ministry it worked wonders. The kids enjoyed the personal attention, and Bible reading became a regular habit in the lives of many of them.

We described this aspect of our own Children's Church ministry in such detail just to illustrate the importance of finding ways to encourage the students to follow through on our teaching, to lead them to become "doers of the word."

Ask Andy!

Dear Andy,

I've been teaching in Children's Church for about three years now, and to be honest, the job has kind of lost its appeal. I used to enjoy preparing the lessons, and I actually used to look forward to Sunday! But not anymore. The zip and sparkle are gone.

Here's my question: Do I quit and hope they can find somebody else, keep plugging away, or what? I used to think that God called me to this ministry, but now I'm not really sure.

Tara Dactyl

Dear Tara,

What you just described is often referred to as "burnout." They say it happens to everyone. Once the new wears off, teaching is plain old hard work. What used to be a delight can quickly become drudgery.

At this point, you have three options: (1) continue as you are, enduring the position and doing enough to get by, which isn't good for you or the students; (2) resign, which is definitely the wrong choice if God has called you and wants you there; (3) "re-sign." Ask God to give you a new vision for the work He has chosen for you, a new love and burden for the kids, a new enthusiasm for the class.

Plan some outings and opportunities to have some fun with your kids; read and study and look for ways to improve your teaching skills; promise the Lord that with

His help you'll do your very best.

It's up to you—maintain, resign or "re-sign." I trust that you'll make the right choice.

Andy

Dear Andy,

It happened again, and I'm about to go bananas! The Christian school teachers are always using our Children's Church equipment and supplies, but this time they've gone too far! I bought this new extension cord and labeled it "Property of Children's Church—Do Not Use!" (I purposely got a bright blue one—different from all the others in the church so they would notice it wasn't theirs.)

But it didn't make any difference. Someone used it, and apparently couldn't find an adapter, so they broke off the third prong!

If this was the first time, I guess I could find it in my heart to forgive, but this is probably the millionth time!

They use our dry-marker pens and leave the caps off. They "borrow" our tape and forget to put it back. Once they even loaned our overhead projector to another school, and we didn't find out until Sunday!

Enough is enough! Can you help us?

Iva Hadit

Dear Iva,

I understand your frustration, but this is an excellent opportunity to put Ephesians 4:32 into practice. Anytime two or more ministries use the same facilities, some misunderstandings and friction are sure to result, and there will be a tremendous need for communication and cooperation. When you consider that so many different people have access to the classrooms, it's hard to put the blame for the "borrowing" on just one group.

If possible, it's usually best for each group that uses the classroom to have their own cabinets or supply closet, complete with locks. There's a real satisfaction in knowing that when you open the closet to get the blue extension cord, it's going to be there!

I would also suggest a meeting of the various ministries that use your room. Come to an agreement as to who is responsible for the cleaning and straightening of the room, how the chairs or desks are to be arranged after school Friday and after Children's Church on Sunday, etc.

The first step in overcoming misunderstandings and disagreements is communication!

Andy

Dear Andy,

Help us, please, before one of my staff punches out a Children's Church mother! This woman has to leave for work immediately after the morning service, so she barges into Children's Church every Sunday about twenty minutes before dismissal to get her kids (usually about three minutes before the end of the Bible message). She barges in like she's not even aware that we're having a service. "Yoo-hoo! Lisa! Brandon! Let's go! Get your coats!"

This inconsiderate woman has been doing this for the last two months, and she's driving the other teachers and me crazy. We've tried to talk with her about it, but it's like talking to a Cape buffalo.

Any suggestions?

Art Tillery

Dear Art,

This woman may just be inconsiderate, never having stopped to think about how much distraction she is causing; but then again, she may even be doing it on purpose. But either way, don't punch her out. It's just not the best way to go about things.

By now you should know almost exactly what time this woman is scheduled to make her next appearance. Plan to cancel her next engagement. Seat Brandon and Lisa on the back row so they won't be a distraction as they slip out early. Then have one of your workers slip out with these two about five minutes before Mom comes for them (be sure to get their coats and Bibles). The worker should stand in the hallway with them until Mom shows, just to make sure that they don't wander off or re-enter the Children's Church room.

Many adults just never see the importance of the Children's Church service, and you have to do everything you can to protect it. Hope this helps!

Andy

12.
TIME-FILLERS

It's 12:15, and you're ready to dismiss Children's Church. The Bible review game is finished, and your behavior award winners have just played *The Price Is Right*. Now it's time to pass out the Bible-reading slips and go home.

But just as you're about to dismiss in prayer, one of your workers slips up to you and whispers, "Pastor's getting ready to baptize some folks. We need to hold the kids another ten minutes."

So what do you do for the next ten minutes? The kids are ready to be dismissed, and so are you, but you've got to keep them occupied until you get the "all-clear" from the adult service.

Many Children's Church leaders simply lead songs until they get the dismissal signal. But a song service at this point is usually half-hearted and lifeless. You're simply filling time rather than singing to praise the Lord, and the kids know it. Children's Church ends up on a bad note.

Why not have some brief activities planned for those emergency situations when you're forced to go beyond your scheduled service? These activities can add VARIETY to your program and make the extended time enjoyable rather than a drudgery.

Here are several ideas that teachers have successfully used over the years:

1. Charades. A charade in this sense is a Bible story that is silently acted out. Students become the actors and actresses, while the rest of the class attempts to guess which Bible story is being portrayed.

Select the students that will participate in the charade, then take them from the room and give

No costumes or props are needed.

them simple instructions while your song leader leads the rest of the group in a chorus. When you return to the room with your "cast," instruct the class to remain silent as they watch the charade but to raise one hand when they know which Bible story is being acted out.

When the charade is finished, call on different students to guess which Bible incident was being portrayed. The student who correctly identifies the Bible story becomes an actor/actress in the next charade.

Keep the charades simple, and remember that there are no speaking parts. The students gesture, use facial expressions, and move about, but never speak; no costumes or props are needed. Here are a few simple charades to give you a feel for this activity:

a. David and Goliath (2 boys). The taller of the two boys enters the room and walks to the front of the group. He stands with arms raised, flexing his muscles, as though he is boasting of his great strength. The shorter student enters and approaches the "giant." He reaches into his pocket, pretends to remove a rock and place it in a sling, then twirls it about his head. When he releases one end of the sling, the "giant" claps one hand to his forehead and falls down dead.

This simplest of charades is a good starter. Even the youngest Primaries will not miss which story is being portrayed.

b. Solomon and the baby (2 girls, 3 boys). This charade begins with one boy seated in a chair, with the other two boys standing on each side of him as guards.

The guards stand erect with one fist held out at shoulder height, as though holding a spear. The girls enter the room, one pretending to cradle an infant in her arms.

As the "women" approach the "king," the one snatches the "baby" from the arms of the other, who then snatches it back. The fight continues until the "king" holds out one hand to stop them. He turns to a guard, who draws a "sword" from his belt and hands it to the king. At this point, one woman falls down on her knees before the "king," hands clasped before her as though begging for the life of her baby.

c. Naaman (2 girls, 2 boys). The two girls and one boy enter the room in a tight cluster as though riding in a chariot, with one of the girls driving. The "chariot" crosses the room and stops in front of a classroom door.

"Naaman" climbs down from the chariot and knocks on the door. The second boy opens the door, steps into the room, and points across the room as though telling Naaman to go there. He holds up seven fingers and then steps back into the house and closes the door behind him.

"Naaman" climbs back into the chariot, which then takes him to the river as instructed. He steps from the chariot, wades out into the water, and dips under seven times.

Other charades that have been a lot of fun are *Ananias and Sapphira, The Lame Man at the Temple, Balaam and the Donkey, Adam and Eve* (eating the forbidden fruit), and *The Good Samaritan*. Use your imagination. Many of the familiar Bible stories make good charades.

Charades can be a lot of fun for your students. Plan them in advance. Write out a list of the Bible stories you intend to have your students portray, with the number of male and female actors needed for each. Keep the action simple. Tuck your list away in your wallet or purse, and the next time you are told, "You can't dismiss for fifteen more minutes," you'll be ready with charades!

2. Testimonies. Allow your students to give their salvation testimonies. Instruct them that the testimony should be brief and should include three things: how old they were when they received Jesus as Saviour; where they were (church, home, school, etc.); and how it happened. Start the testimony time by giving your own testimony (briefly), then calling on one or two teachers to give theirs. Once the ice is broken, most students enjoy sharing their testimonies. It's a new experience for many of them!

3. Dollar Drop. This activity has absolutely no spiritual value; it's simply a fun change of pace and can be used on the spur of the moment. One word of warning: it can cost you an occasional dollar!

So I was only six when Jesus saved me!

Crease a dollar bill lengthwise, then reopen it. Ask for a volunteer who would like to earn a dollar, and you'll have plenty of takers. Hold the dollar bill lightly by one end, and have the volunteer place a thumb and forefinger an inch apart on each side of the bill (dead center, in front of George Washington's portrait). Instruct the student to close his thumb and finger quickly when you drop the bill. If he is fast enough to catch the dollar in this way, he can keep it!

Give each volunteer three chances, but caution them about touching the bill before you drop it, which counts as a miss. On the second try, move the bill slightly, but don't drop it. Most kids will grab it, which counts as their second miss. On the third attempt, go ahead and drop the bill again.

As you select volunteers to try the dollar drop, announce that you are searching for the quietest students. Take your time making your selections—the other workers will enjoy the peace and quiet!

Most people (let a worker try occasionally) cannot catch the bill before it slips through their fingers. But there is an occasional volunteer who does, so be prepared to give away the dollar if you try this one.

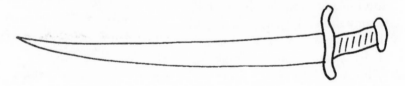

4. **Sword drills.** A "Sword drill" is simply an exercise in finding Scripture passages quickly. The teacher calls, "Draw Swords," and each student responds by raising his Bible over his head with one hand. The teacher gives the Scripture reference twice, then says, "Charge!" The student who finds the passage first stands and begins reading it.

If you desire, divide the students into teams for competition. Give one point for finding the verse, then ask a question from the verse and give one point for a correct answer. Tie the Sword drill into the day's teaching aim by selecting verses that deal with that subject.

5. Favorite songs. Allow five or six students to select their favorite songs for a brief song service. As you announce this, mention the number of students you are choosing and point out that you are selecting quiet students who are participating in the song service.

When the first song comes to an end, select a second student to choose the next song. If properly conducted, a song time of favorites can be an orderly, meaningful time, even though the kids are restless and ready to be dismissed.

6. Scripture puzzles. On the chalkboard or dry erase board, draw the appropriate number of blanks for a brief key phrase from Scripture such as, "Seek ye first the kingdom of God," "But be ye doers of the Word," "Ye shall be witnesses unto me," etc. Beneath the blanks draw a score box on one side, and a bomb with an extremely long fuse on the other.

The puzzle is played hangman-style. Alternate between the two teams, allowing students to guess letters in the puzzle and filling in the correct letters guessed.

Give one point for each letter as it appears in the phrase. If a letter is guessed that does not appear in the phrase, light the fuse on the bomb, allowing it to burn even further for each incorrect guess.

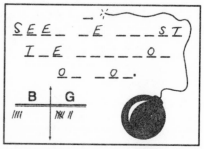

7. Short stories. If you have a master storyteller among your Children's Church teachers, key him or her always to be ready with an exciting short story. When you don't have a staff member who is willing to accept such a challenge, keep a book of short, exciting missionary stories on hand. On the occasion when you need a time-filler, have a teacher (who reads with expression) read one of the stories.

When you unexpectedly find out that the adult service is going into overtime and you must hold the kids for another fifteen minutes, it need not be a time for panic. Always be ready with a few "time-fillers" that you have prepared in advance. As with the other parts of your Children's

Church program, use VARIETY even when choosing your "time-fillers." If you're properly prepared, your students will enjoy this unexpected part of Children's Church.

Ask Andy!

Dear Andy,

I just started teaching in Children's Church, and I love it! The kids are fantastic. We're going to have some good times together. I'm looking forward to teaching them about the Lord and maybe seeing some of them get saved.

I've never taught before, and I just wanted to ask what I should do to learn how. I have a basic idea of how to go about it, but I also know that I have a lot to learn. I want to do my very best—for my Lord and for my kids.

Can you help me?

Tim Burr

Dear Tim,

Congratulations on your new teaching position! You're in for a lot of blessings, trials, thrills and hard work. I like your attitude. Always give your very, very best to this ministry.

To answer your question—yes, there are some things that you can do to improve your teaching ministry. Any teacher, novice or veteran, needs to be constantly seeking to sharpen his teaching skills. A teacher who has stopped learning is on the way down.

Start by asking your pastor or Christian Education Director to recommend some good books, videos, and/or filmstrips that will help develop your teaching abilities. There are books and videos on various teaching methods, how to make and use visual aids, age-group characteristics, etc.

One of the best ways to learn and grow as a teacher is to read.

A second source of information and encouragement is other teachers. I've learned many valuable teaching tips by watching other teachers who work with Primaries and Juniors. (Sometimes you even learn what *not* to do!)

Is there a teacher in your church who is really outstanding with kids? Visit her class two or three Sundays and take some notes. You might even visit a school classroom or two. I once made a twelve-hour trip to another state just to watch a man who had an outstanding Children's Church ministry. It was worth the trip!

One final suggestion—have a friend videotape Children's Church for three or four Sundays. Watch the tapes after church for a self-evaluation. This can be a bit intimidating, but it gives you an honest, unbiased evaluation of your teaching! Target the weaknesses that you observe on the tape and work to improve those areas of your ministry.

Thanks for writing. You've just embarked on a teaching adventure that will touch many lives for eternity. Never lose your teachable attitude, and always give your very best!

Andy

A FINAL WORD

On May 22, 1915, a lonely little spot known as Quintinshill became the scene of the worst disaster in British railway history. Two railway men, George Meakin and James Tinsley, grew careless in their duties for a moment or two. Their lack of attention to responsibility resulted in a three-train collision that claimed well over two hundred lives.

Quintinshill was a "block post" with lay-by loops on both the north- and southbound lines. At 6:30 a.m. James Tinsley arrived on the northbound local train to take over station duties from George Meakin, who had worked the night shift. Meakin switched the local to the southbound tracks to allow a faster northbound express to travel through, *but failed to set the proper warning signals.*

Tinsley took over from Meakin and began making entries in the Train Register. He was interrupted by a call from Kirkpatrick, the block post to the north, asking line-clear for a southbound troop train. Even though the southbound tracks were occupied by the train on which he had just arrived, which was standing just yards from his station, *Tinsley gave the all-clear.* Moments later as the bell rang signaling that the train had entered the Quintinshill section, *Tinsley again rang all-clear.*

The troop train, loaded with 485 soldiers and officers of the 1st/7th Royal Scots, thundered toward Quintinshill at 70 m.p.h. As the engine roared down a gradient and passed beneath a bridge, the horrified engineer and fireman saw the engine of the local facing them on their own line. The speeding troop train slammed into the stationary local with an impact that was heard for miles.

The force of the collision hurled the local backwards forty yards. The carriages of the troop train, twisting and splintering, hurled their bulk into the wreckage and sprawled across the parallel northbound track. The train's length of 213 yards was reduced to less than seventy yards.

Meakin and Tinsley stared in horror at the spectacle, then suddenly remembered the northbound express. Meakin made a dash for the levers to set the danger signals, *but he was too late.* Moments later the express thundered into the station to slam into the wreckage of the other two trains. Gas cylinders fueling the lamps of the coaches exploded into flame, creating a blazing inferno, as trapped passengers screamed in anguish.

A reporter on the scene wrote later: "When the awful force of the second collision burst upon the troop train, engines were heaped on one another, carriages telescoped and overturned. Men were pinned helplessly beneath them. The carriage doors were jammed, and scarlet flames belched from the blazing interior. As dawn was breaking the bird chorus mingled ghoulishly with screams of human anguish. It was an unbearable experience."

The results of a moment or two of carelessness were unbelievable: 239 dead, exactly 300 injured, many of them seriously. Many of those who survived would go through life as amputees.

James Tinsley received a three-year prison sentence, and George Meakin was given eighteen months. The carelessness of these two men would impact hundreds of lives for many years to come. Their lack of responsibility had resulted in tragedy.

May we as Children's Church teachers never fail to recognize the awesome responsibility that has been placed upon us as we teach the eternal truths of God's Word! Failure to carry out our responsibilities can result in tragedy.

The purpose of *"I Can't Wait Till Sunday Morning!"* is to encourage you in your ministry to the children, to challenge you to seek to improve your teaching skills, and to motivate you always to give your very best. I've tried to challenge you to use a VARIETY of teaching methods and visual aids. I've encouraged you to spend time with your students, visiting in their homes and taking them on outings and activities. I've shared ideas for lesson plans and Bible review games and behavior contests.

Will this book make a difference in your Children's Church ministry? Will you incorporate some of the ideas and suggestions that were presented here to enhance your teaching ministry? Will your Children's Church sparkle and shine with VARIETY as you try some new approaches to teaching? Will you accept a challenge to learn, grow, and sharpen your communication skills? It's up to you.

If this book has pointed out some needs in your Children's Church ministry, or given you some fresh ideas, or motivated you to make some positive changes, follow through on those right away. Make some notes right now while the ideas are fresh. Get started making that new Bible game right away. Call the church handyman this evening to ask if he can make some *Let's Make a Deal* boxes. Draw up a Children's Church visitation schedule this evening.

This book will do you absolutely no good unless you follow through on the ideas that were presented. The success of this writing is not measured in terms of how many new ideas were presented, but rather by how much you do.

God bless you in your ministry to the children, "the greatest in the kingdom of heaven"!

The Children's Church Teacher's Checklist

Yes, No, I   I
I Do Don't Will

___ ___ ___   1. I see my ministry as a calling from God and attempt to give my best.

___ ___ ___   2. I visit regularly in the homes of my students.

___ ___ ___   3. I'm developing a loving, personal relationship with each student.

___ ___ ___   4. I pray daily for my students.

___ ___ ___   5. I plan monthly outings and activities.

___ ___ ___   6. I use a VARIETY of teaching methods.

___ ___ ___   7. I use a VARIETY of visual aids.

___ ___ ___   8. I prepare my lesson early in the week.

___ ___ ___   9. I make certain that my lesson is on the child's level, using appropriate illustrations and familiar terminology.

___ ___ ___ 10. I develop my lesson around a specific teaching aim.

___ ___ ___ 11. I integrate my teaching aim into all parts of the teaching hour.

___ ___ ___ 12. I find tangible ways to encourage my students to put the lesson into action.